Dear Cindy,
It has been great
to meet you and we
truly pray that our
paths will cross again
holds you and your country
up in prayer at this time.

We

god bless!
Tick and Tocin

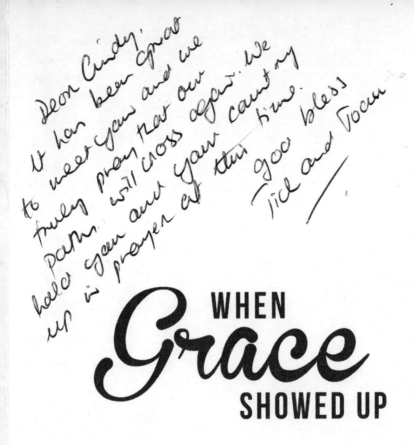

WHEN
Grace
SHOWED UP

WHEN
Grace
SHOWED UP

ONE COUPLE'S STORY OF HOPE AND HEALING
AMONG THE POOR

TICH *and* JOAN SMITH
WITH LIZA HOEKSMA

David C Cook®
transforming lives together

WHEN GRACE SHOWED UP
Published by David C Cook
4050 Lee Vance View
Colorado Springs, CO 80918 U.S.A.

David C Cook U.K., Kingsway Communications
Eastbourne, East Sussex BN23 6NT, England

The graphic circle C logo is a registered trademark of David C Cook.

LCCN 2016938480
ISBN 978-1-4347-1031-4
eISBN 978-1-4347-1086-4

The Cook Team: Kyle Duncan, Ian Matthews, Amy Konyndyk, Nick Lee,
Jon Middel, Helen Macdonald, Tiffany Thomas, Susan Murdock
Cover Design: Leigh Jameson
Cover Photo: Carita McCririe

Printed and bound by CPI Group (UK) Ltd, Croydon, CR0 4YY
First Edition 2016

1 2 3 4 5 6 7 8 9 10

052716

We dedicate this book to family.

To our Father in heaven who loved us so much you gave us your Son, Jesus, that we might have life, and your Holy Spirit, our ever present Helper, who continues to teach us and guide us along the narrow path, encouraging us to walk by faith and not by sight.

To our parents, Gerald and Peggy Smith, Bunty and Billie Waring, for your unconditional love and always believing in us.

To our siblings, Guy and Sue, Felicity and Amanda, for standing by us through the good and bad times.

To Sue and Vin, for giving us the most wonderful children.

To our children and their spouses, Julie and Andrew, Greg and Kirst, Grant and Kate, Katie and Curtis, for your love and patience with us, and your unconditional support. We honour you and are so proud of who you are.

To our eight beautiful grandchildren,
Sebastian and Luca; Anna, Tommy and
Molly; Baby Billi; Ben and Jack, each one
of you, unique and special, blessings beyond
what we could have thought or imagined.

To our LIV family. A special gift from heaven in
our twilight years. To every LIV child, and every
mother and co-worker, what a privilege to be your
Mkhulu and Gogo, and Baba and Mama, as we
continue to journey together to rescue, restore, raise
and release the precious children of our nation.

Thank you, one and all, for enriching our lives.
You inspire us to continue to go further, love deeper,
and believe for the much more that is yet to come.

We are family. Together we can.

Our prayer is that you, our readers, will also be
encouraged to go further, love deeper, leave the
comfort of the harbour, step out of the boat, dare
to imagine, and believe for the impossible.

In Jesus, all things are possible.

CONTENTS

FOREWORD

I love Tich and Joan Smith. I love LIV. And I love this story. As the title suggests it is a story of God's grace from beginning to end. It is also the story of a couple approaching a comfortable retirement who were ambushed by God and used by him to bring transformation, hope and healing to many lives.

I visit LIV every year and the village is a taste of heaven. It never ceases to inspire me. It is an oasis of love and joy in the midst of a desert of pain, hopelessness and despair. Tich and Joan have both known brokenness, pain and despair in their own lives and it is just like God to take this couple and, in their vulnerability, make his power perfect in their weakness.

This book is a story of amazing miracles. I would never have thought when I met Tich and Joan in the township of Amaoti on a hot and dusty day all those years ago that the Lord would create the story you are about to read. God sneaked up on them and broke their hearts over the plight of the orphaned, the abandoned and the abused children of Africa. The Scripture tells us that "those who sow in tears will reap in joy". Well, there has indeed been much sowing in tears.

We have wept together over many who have been taken by AIDS or violence at what should have been the beginning of their lives. There are still tears but now there is also much reaping in joy as Tich and Joan and their amazing team see so many lives transformed by the love of Jesus.

I am conflicted as I write this. On the one hand I want to tell you that the Smiths are a very ordinary couple who have known pain and despair and walk with a limp. I want to tell you that their story can be your story because it is simply about two people discovering that God's grace really is enough. But at the same time I want to tell you that my friends really are extraordinary as this is also true. They are an ordinary couple who keep saying "yes" to Jesus; that is what makes them extraordinary. They said yes to loving hundreds and hundreds of children in a costly and sacrificial way. They take incredible risks of faith when they believe God has spoken to them. And they are amazingly obedient. I could go on and talk about their generosity, humility, courage and persistence; that would be all true as well.

However, they would say that this story is not first and foremost about them. It is not even primarily about the children whose lives are being transformed in miraculous ways. It is a story which is, from beginning to end, about the Lord Jesus who loves us, who died to save us and who rose again to give us the power to usher in his kingdom, his rule and his reign in some of the most broken and forsaken places.

This is a story of hope. Read on and be inspired to live wholeheartedly for Jesus and see what he can do as you say "yes" to him.

Mike Pilavachi
Soul Survivor

ACKNOWLEDGEMENTS

Dr. Zweli Mkhize, for embracing a white man, with a funny name like Tich, and believing in his crazy vision to build villages across our land, that South Africa will one day become known as a country who looks after their children to the glory of Jesus Christ. Thank you for taking a huge step of faith, and for being the man of integrity that we have come to know and respect, and love as a friend and family.

Government, business and the church, for trusting us and partnering with us, as, together, we change our nation, one child at a time.

Mike Pilavachi, for your friendship and encouragement along the way, and for pushing us to write the story so that others will be encouraged to go and be his hands and feet.

Liza, we gave you an impossible task to help us write the story. We have laughed and cried together, and wrestled at times, but we have loved every minute of the journey with you. You are now officially part of the LIV family.

David C Cook, if you hadn't believed in the story and taken a leap of faith, this wouldn't have been written. We have loved working with you and getting to know you.

Peter, Rory, Felicity and Ann, for mentoring us, and never giving up on us, and to the many others who have sown into our lives.

Our Prayer Warriors, who keep praying, standing shoulder to shoulder with us, and the whole LIV team, as we rebuild the broken walls of young lives.

The LIV board members, and governors, for your wisdom, friendship, patience and perseverance with us. We continue to walk together with courage and growing faith in our Provider.

INTRODUCTION

Rescue. Restore. Raise. Release.

Imagine a village in Durban, South Africa, in the heart of the Zulu kingdom, where you hear the laughter of children as the sun rises. A place of faith, hope, justice and love; a place where lives are being transformed; a place that orphans can call home.

Imagine vulnerable children given a safe home, food to eat, parents to nurture them, and a school to educate them. Imagine thousands of children rescued from desperate neglect, abuse and poverty, raised to know they have a Father in heaven who loves them.

Imagine the restoration of the family with Jesus Christ in the centre. Imagine abandoned children placed in a loving community, raised to be the leaders of tomorrow, and released to shine like stars.

Imagine a self-sustaining village, supporting a thousand children, offering skills development and jobs for the rural communities. Imagine a solution to an overwhelming problem, and a government asking why it works and discovering the answer is Jesus.

You'd think God would have put his best people on a project like that. You'd think he'd handpick a strong man and woman of faith, intelligent and wise with an unblemished record.

But he didn't. He chose us, two cracked pots called Tich and Joan Smith. Maybe no one else was foolish enough to say yes to such a crazy idea. He gave us a vision; one we knew we could never make happen in our own strength, but one that would call us to rely on him every step of the way. How could we say anything but "yes" to the God who had rescued us from so much? How could we not obey the call to love others as he has loved us?

This book tells the story of LIV—Lungisisa Indlela Village—but more importantly it tells a story of what God can do through ordinary lives. He can take each of us, with our strengths and weaknesses, our dreams and desires, our fears and failures, and he can use us to transform even the darkest of places. He started with some incredibly raw materials in us but, when grace showed up and we said yes to him, he took us on an adventure that has been far more than we could ever have dared to ask or imagine. Our intention for writing this book was not so that you might think we're something special; we're not. Our hope and prayer is that as you read some of the things that Jesus has done in our lives, you will be encouraged to lay down your life before him again, and that you would have your eyes opened to the adventure he wants to take you on. It may be risky, it may cost you all you have, but we guarantee it will be absolutely worth it.

So we invite you to journey with us from a place where we were both so broken and so desperate that we thought there was no reason to live, to being rescued by God, restored, raised and released that we might be a blessing to others and God might be glorified.

Journey with us and see God's vision to turn one of South Africa's biggest problems into a solution that could change the country. Come and find out why it takes a village to raise a child.

PART I

Rescued and Restored

Chapter 1

TICH'S STORY

God ... set me apart from my mother's
womb and called me by his grace.

Galatians 1:15

When I met Jesus, my life was in a mess. I was in the gutter. I had wrecked my marriage and had been a terrible father to my two beautiful children. I was crippled with addictions, had no job, no home and no future. My glittering sporting career was long over. I had chased fame and fortune and discovered it was just a mirage. Jumping from a rooftop and ending my own life seemed a real option. I thought that there was nothing left in this world for me, no reason to live.

I should never have been able to play cricket or rugby; in fact, I shouldn't have been able to walk at all. When I was six years old one of my favourite tricks was to walk along the outside windowsill of my bedroom. We lived in a double storey house so my dad had warned me more than once not to do it as it was dangerous. One afternoon I was showing off in front of my sister, Sue's, friends, when she closed the window I was about to climb back through. As I turned around to find another way back inside, I slipped and fell, landing in a sprawling heap two storeys below. I screamed in agony and my mum came out to find me with my leg sticking out at a right angle to my body. I had broken my hip.

She rushed me to hospital and after surgery the doctors said that I may never be able to walk or run again. I was too young to take in the significance of those words; all I remember was spending three months in traction at the children's hospital in Johannesburg. The break was so severe that even when I was discharged I had to wear a plaster cast from my toes up to my chest for six long months. When that came off, a miracle healing had taken place and the doctors were amazed I was able to walk and run just as I had before. It wasn't long before I was back playing soccer, rugby and cricket with my brother, Guy, in the back yard.

SPORT

Sport had always been the centre of our lives, and it was the god in our home, with Guy and me following in Dad's footsteps and discovering a love for cricket and rugby. When I was picked for my first cricket team at the age of seven (the under-10 team that Guy captained) I was only as big as the stumps. Mum and Dad had named me Anthony John Shaw Smith but I soon earned the nickname Tich because I was so tiny—a full head shorter than all of my classmates. I became known around the local Johannesburg schools as "a tiny fella with a lot of sporting talent".

Roger Prideaux (the former Northants and England opening batsman) was my first professional coach at school and I clearly remember him writing on the back of my treasured cricket bat, "You can play for South Africa if you practise really hard. Work really hard!" That message stuck in my head and was a real encouragement to me as a young boy, spurring me on to give sport my all. I was trained by a number of professional coaches from England, including the famous umpire Dickie Bird, John Hurry and Johnny Waite (the former South African wicketkeeper). I was chosen for the local provincial cricket teams from a young age and participated in the renowned Nuffield Cricket Tournament for three years, culminating in being chosen for the South African schools XI in 1968.

I played fly-half in the school rugby teams throughout my school days. Sport was my first love and I trained and practised extremely hard. This seemed to pay dividends and many tipped me for greater things when I left school. Though I was consumed by the love of sport, there was another passion that was ignited in my final year. My uncle John was chairman at Turffontein Racecourse and I remember going there with my dad at my uncle's invitation. My dad gave me R10 (around £5/$7) to bet with and that first day at the racecourse I won R300—about the cost of a second-hand car. My family never had much money and we were not spoiled with the material things of life, so it was a huge win. It was my first experience of gambling and I liked the taste of it!

MILITARY TRAINING

In those days in South Africa, it was compulsory for young men to do a year's military training on leaving school as there were terrorist wars on some of our northern borders. A group of 27 of us travelled from the Nuffield Cricket Tournament to the Air Force Gymnasium in Pretoria to do our military training. The Air Force Gym was a haven for top sportsmen in a number of sports, with rugby, athletics and cricket taking priority. After basic training, the soldiers were sent to bases around the country to complete their military training, and many of them experienced combat on the border. Due to our sporting ability, we were encouraged to do the instructors' course, so that we could stay in Pretoria and be able to focus on sport, training the new recruits who came in the half yearly in-take group.

My parents' house was only 30 minutes from the Air Force Gym, so when we got weekend passes we headed there. At times there were up to 16 of us chucking down mattresses on the floor to crash after a heavy night of drinking and partying. My parents might not have had much money but they certainly had a special gift for hospitality! It was the first time we were legally old enough to drink and we slipped very easily into the partying, womanising and clubbing scene in Johannesburg.

UNIVERSITY LIFE

When my year in the Air Force was up, I wanted to go and play cricket in England, but my dad insisted that I go to university to get some education behind me before I embarked on a sporting career. Dad never had the privilege of going to university because he went to serve in the South African Air Force during World War II and he was adamant that his boys would have every opportunity that he didn't have.

The freedom of university sucked me in and my priorities were totally upside down. I was interested in sport, partying, girls and academics, in that order. With so much time committed to the first three on that list, there was little time for study. I started to play fly-half[1] for the Natal (state) under-20 team when I was 18 and we had the incredible privilege of playing in the main curtain-raiser games to three of the four rugby tests between the South African national team, the Springboks, and the world famous New Zealand All Blacks in 1970. It was an amazing experience to play at these test grounds before large crowds and get a taste of what it would be like to play at the highest level. By the time I was 19, I was playing fly-half for Natal under the captaincy of former Springbok captain Tommy Bedford. We played against England at the Kings Park Stadium in Durban before 44,000 people; what an exhilarating experience for a young guy!

My rugby career came to an abrupt end after I hurt my knee during a cricket game and had to have a serious cartilage operation. It was gutting to let go of a game that I loved but I focused on my cricket and, the following year, I was chosen to play for Natal, and the year after for the South African cricket team.

I remember my first cricket game for Natal so clearly. It was a friendly against North-Eastern Transvaal in Pretoria and I kept wicket really well with six dismissals in my first innings as well as getting some runs. I remember waking up the next morning to see the headline in the Sunday paper, "'Tiny Tich' is 6ft. star". I was elated.

---

1   Similar to a quarterback in American football.

In those days there was no live television coverage so we played in front of full houses at many of our stadiums. South Africa is sport mad; we were treated like gods wherever we went and we hugely enjoyed our celebrity status. Everything was done for us from the booking of air tickets to arrangements to stay at five-star hotels. Everywhere we went children would line up wanting autographs, we had frequent press coverage, and women made themselves freely available; there were temptations at every turn and I fell head first into it all. The fame and lifestyle was intoxicating and I look back and cringe at the arrogance that the attention bred in me. I lapped it up, believing the hype and thinking that the world owed me a living. I became so self-centred and I thought that I was something special just because I could play sport. Little did I know that once you put down the bat and the ball you're just the same as the person next to you. It's your character that makes you special not what you can do on the sports field.

APARTHEID

Had I lived in another era, I would have been playing cricket around the world, but two years before I got picked for the South African team our country was banned from all international sport. The sporting world had recognised the horrendous way the South African government had segregated the races using the apartheid system and refused to allow us to take part in any international sport until apartheid was abolished. People of colour could not play sport with white people and were not even allowed to watch sport alongside them. I so clearly remember the demarcated areas which only allowed about a thousand people of colour to watch the games, segregated from the rest of the spectators. Though this made me uneasy, to my shame I never questioned the status quo. For us, apartheid was something that we were born into; we didn't know anything else and it just became a way of life. I had no interest in politics and no real comprehension of how wrong and immoral this system was. Anyone who stood up against apartheid was considered a terrorist and a threat to our country's security and almost all of them ended up in jail. The majority of us thought it was best to ignore the situation and get on with life as we knew it. I am deeply saddened that I did not do more to change this horrific era in our history.

Even as sportsmen, keen to play at the highest level, we simply accepted that our teams were banned from international sport as we knew the white South African government were not going to change their minds. South Africa did, however, entertain "rebel tours" that were not acknowledged by sporting bodies around the world and those who played in them risked being given a life ban. I was fortunate enough to play for South Africa in an unofficial three match series against an English invitational team called the Derek Robins XI.

One of the highlights of my career was when the International Wanderers team toured South Africa and played three unofficial tests against a strong South African national team which, for the first time, included three players of colour. The International Wanderers team was possibly one of the strongest cricket teams to visit our shores and included household names of international cricketers from both England and Australia. That team included Dennis Lillee, Ian and Greg Chappell, Gary Gilmour, Bob Taylor, Alan Knott, Derek Underwood,

Alan Hurst, Dennis Amiss, Tony Greig, Bob Woolmer and others. A very competitive series resulted in us sharing the series one-all.

I was a youngster at the time and Dennis Lillee wrote in his autobiography that I was one of the best young players of fast bowling that he had bowled against. It was a great compliment from a man considered by many to be the best fast bowler of his era.

With my attention so much on my sport, it's no wonder that I walked away from university without a degree, despite retaking my final year. I really let my folks down as they had sacrificed a lot to put me and my brother through university. At least Guy worked far harder than me and qualified as a lawyer.

FAMILY LIFE

I left South Africa in 1974 to play cricket in England for Middlesex. It was an incredible experience, though I had to play in the 2nd XI and for the under-25s as they were only allowed to play two international players per team. I was offered a three-year contract by one of the other English counties, but I refused it as I'd had an offer of a job in South Africa. One of the influential people in my cricket career, Johnny Waite (the former South Africa wicketkeeper), offered to finance a sports shop in Pietermaritzburg where I would be a 50 per cent shareholder. It seemed like too good an opportunity for me to pass up so I returned home to start my business career.

This also meant that I was reunited with my university sweetheart, Sue. As the university Rag Queen,[2] she was strikingly beautiful and she

---

2   Beauty Queen.

was a woman of high moral values who wanted a simple family life. We got married when I was 24 and Sue was 23, our beautiful daughter Julie arriving not long after in July 1976. Two years later our family was complete when our son Greg was born. I loved my family, but I was still incredibly self-absorbed. My life continued to be consumed with sport, gambling, partying and drinking. I was frequently away on cricket tours but even when I was home my life revolved around my other interests. Every Wednesday and Saturday I would go to the horse races and often came home late at night, very drunk. Some nights I didn't even make it home. Like many addicts I couldn't see that my gambling and drinking were a problem.

John 12:35 says, "Whoever walks in the dark does not know where they are going." That was me. I was so caught up in the darkness that I couldn't see how my behaviour was impacting those I loved. I lived a life where I thought the world revolved around me and me alone. Now I look back and deeply regret the way I treated Sue and my children; a more self-centred, egotistical lifestyle is difficult to imagine.

LOSING MY INSPIRATION

My dad was by far the biggest influence in my sporting career. It was he who had built cricket nets in the back garden so Guy and I could practise, he who challenged and inspired me to keep training and aim high. He always used to say to me that you could not count yourself as a cricketer unless you had scored a hundred at the Boxing Day game in Johannesburg where the two strongest provinces, Transvaal and Natal, would play each other. I'd never seen him so proud as on

Boxing Day 1975 when he came into the changing rooms after I scored my first, first class hundred.

A few years after Sue and I got married, Dad started to have trouble with the muscles in his hands and he was eventually diagnosed with motor neurone disease. The illness started to eat away at his muscles until he couldn't work any longer. One of my old school mates, Tommy Lee, phoned me to say that he heard Dad was sick and to ask my permission to go and pray with him. "Do what you want," I replied, not believing for a second that it would make any difference. My dad wasn't healed physically but Tommy did lead him to Jesus, and he was healed spiritually. I will be forever grateful to Tommy because Dad went home to be with Jesus 18 months later.

I always say that Dad was one of the fortunate ones because most people die by surprise. As this dreaded disease wore my dad down, he became frightened, and it was in this place of vulnerability that he gave his life to Jesus. Despite the terrible effects motor neurone disease had on his body, he never missed church on a Sunday and he fell passionately in love with Jesus, something I couldn't comprehend at the time. When he was dying in hospital, he asked my family not to tell me because I was playing an important cricket match against Western Province. As soon as the game finished and I heard the news, I flew up to Johannesburg and raced to the clinic. I managed to get there in time to spend the last 20 minutes of his life holding his hand and saying goodbye.

I loved my dad and his death hit me hard. Until he was gone, I'd never realised that all my life I'd been playing sport for him. My desire to play waned and my life started to spiral downhill rapidly. I was drinking more than ever and couldn't stay away from the racecourse and the casinos. I had never been dropped in my entire career and eventually at the age of 32, it happened. I decided to call it quits and retired. Without the focus of sport and the need to train and stay fit, my drinking and gambling took an ever stronger hold on my undisciplined life. I was leading a double life, telling Sue that I was away on business trips when instead I would drive for hours to get to the nearest casino and waste days and thousands of rand at the Black Jack tables. Friends noticed that I was gambling and drinking more than ever before but, when they challenged me, I was in denial. I thought alcoholics were people that slept on park benches drinking methylated spirits. That wasn't me. I didn't drink in the mornings and I was a social drinker so therefore I thought I didn't have a problem.

THE FINAL STRAW

Of course, it was a horrific time for Sue who was trying to bring up two young children while her husband was lost in his own world. When I won at the races we had money to spare but when I lost, things got desperate. On more than one occasion she had to deal with the sheriff of the court coming to attach our furniture, taking it in payment of our unpaid accounts. Sue hated owing money so I was putting her through what she described as "hell on earth".

I had to close the sports shop that should have been such a good business because I had gambled the money away. It seems crazy now but I honestly couldn't see what I was putting my family through. I thought that I was being a reasonable husband and father but I cringe when I look back and see how selfishly I behaved. I lived by the "11th commandment"—that I could do what I wanted as long as nobody found out. I never gave the consequences of my behaviour a second thought. The biggest regret of my life is that I treated Sue and my children as I did during those years where I was largely absent.

I thought myself invincible and would drive when I was drunk without considering anyone's safety, having three car accidents whilst under the influence. One time I was pulled over by the police after a day at the races and I literally fell out of the car because I was so wasted. The police officers recognised me, put me in their van and drove me back to my home in Pietermaritzburg 50 kilometres away. They didn't press charges but rather than it making me realise I'd had a lucky escape, this only added to my feelings of being indestructible.

Another time I was driving back to Pietermaritzburg after a heavy afternoon's drinking at the races when I ploughed into a lorry which had stopped on the highway. I was unconscious when they pulled me out of the wreckage. A friend recognised my car, saw me lying lifelessly in silver paper on the side of the road and they called my family to say that they thought that I had been killed on the highway. I woke up in the operating theatre at the hospital and everyone was amazed that I had survived this horrific accident. My brother wouldn't allow me to see the wreckage as the canopy of the bakkie[3] had been ripped off. If I had been a couple of inches to the left, I would have been decapitated. Cold shivers run down my spine when I think that two of my production managers should have been riding in the car with me. Thankfully they chose to catch a train

---

3   A small open-backed truck.

back to Pietermaritzburg instead of coming to the races with me, and their lives were spared. Yet even such a close brush with death wasn't enough to bring me to my senses and stop me drinking.

Despite gambling the sports shop away, I had managed to start a sign writing business which made the signs for all the sports grounds and racecourses in KwaZulu-Natal. This was possible because of the relationships that I had built up over the years mainly through my sporting contacts. I went up to Johannesburg with my sign writers to paint a fleet of trucks for a friend of mine, but whilst the sign writers were painting the trucks, I drew all the money I had left in the business account and went to Newmarket Racecourse. I blew the lot. When I got home to Pietermaritzburg, Sue asked me for some money to pay the bills and once again I had to tell her I had nothing to give. It was the final straw and that Sunday she told me that our marriage was finished; she couldn't take any more and wanted a divorce.

I was devastated. In my naivety I asked how this could happen to me. Divorce only happened to other people. Surely I was not such a bad husband or father? I had always talked my way out of the difficult situations I came up against but this time I knew that there was something different. Sue had taken more than most women could ever have handled and I had finally pushed her to the limit. I didn't know what to do and I drove around Pietermaritzburg in a daze. I found myself on my knees in a Catholic church, all alone, crying out to God to help me and to save my marriage. I had never given God a thought when I was gambling, drinking and womanising, but now, when I had no hope and thought I was about to lose the wife and children that I loved, I found myself crying out to him.

A few days later, I was given a shady "business" opportunity to make R500,000 through an illicit diamond deal. It seemed like the answer to all my worries; my debt would be gone, I would be able to provide for my children, Sue would forgive and forget, and everything would be back to normal. I thought God had answered my prayers. As I sat at the bar of a five-star hotel in Johannesburg where the exchange of the uncut diamonds was to happen and I saw the guys arrive, I had a vision of my two children looking at me through prison bars. I came to my senses, got up and walked out immediately and knew that far from setting up this opportunity for me, this God had actually rescued me from doing something I would always regret.

A FATHER WHO LOVED ME

My brother, Guy, asked me to see a psychologist friend of his, who said that he felt my dependence on alcohol was my biggest problem. He recommended I go to a home for alcoholics and drug addicts and my main reason for agreeing was that I was still desperate to save my marriage. I hoped that Sue would think that I was taking my problems seriously and she would change her mind about the divorce. Just before I went into the home, a friend suggested that I chat to Peter Pollock, a well-known South African cricketer. I knew that I needed help but I didn't know what that help looked like. I went to see Peter and told him my story and he said, "Your life is in such a mess and there is only one answer: his name is Jesus Christ."

I had never thought about following Christ before. I had adopted my beloved dad's motto that it was fine for other people to believe so long as they didn't try and push it down anyone else's throat. I'd been confirmed at the age of 13, a religious ceremony that was part and parcel of going to a Methodist school. For the first time, at the age of 35, I was given an invitation to know Jesus personally. I was told that God loved me just as I was and that he had forgiven me for all that I had done. To someone who felt as messed up and broken as I did, it was life-changing news. I cried my eyes out in Peter's office as I gave my life to Jesus, desperately hoping that he would help me. I wanted this Jesus to wave a magic wand and make everything OK; I had no idea what following him would mean.

I went to Lu Lama, the home for alcoholics and drug addicts, for a month, but when I came out Sue was still adamant that our marriage was over. I hit rock bottom. I was so ashamed of the way that I had hurt my family and let people down that I ran away from all these problems and debts that I had incurred and went to Johannesburg. I got a job selling insurance for race horses. That meant that I was back in the racing crowd, spending time with my old friends who were owners, trainers and jockeys. This inevitably resulted in me returning to the race tracks which soon led to visiting casinos again. My gambling and drinking were worse than ever; I borrowed money and got into even more debt.

Though I had given my life to Jesus, I had never set foot in a church service or read a Bible. I had no Christian friends to help and guide me and I was an absolute mess. Peter Pollock heard that my lifestyle was worse than ever. He continued to pray for me each day but didn't confront me about my behaviour because he felt God tell him, "Leave Tich alone and watch what I will do with this broken life."

One day, as I walked off Germiston Racecourse after trying to organise a betting coup (the horse that we backed came second) and losing money that I couldn't afford, I heard someone say to me, "Go back to Durban to be closer to your children. Get a job, pay back your debt and let people see that your life has changed." I turned around to see who had spoken to me and there was no one there. I packed my bags and headed straight back to Durban, but I couldn't find a job.

Unsurprisingly, no one wanted to employ a broken-down, alcoholic gambler. I had burned many bridges by borrowing money from friends that I couldn't repay. I found a flat at Umdloti, a holiday resort north of Durban, but I couldn't afford any furniture except for a mattress on the floor. When it was my turn to have Julie and Greg for weekends from boarding school, I would take them to stay with friends as the flat wasn't suitable for them and I was so ashamed for them to see the state that I was in. I had hoped to restore my marriage but it was not to be.

I felt that there was nothing left. What was there to live for? I couldn't see any way out of this mess that I was in and I contemplated suicide. Many times I thought about jumping off a building and not having to deal with the chaos I had created. I could see no way out and no hope for my future. I had made a complete mess of my life and—thanks to the success of my sporting career—my demise was fairly public. I was so ashamed of my failures and how I had let everybody down, especially my children. Thankfully I didn't have the courage to take my life and the only thing that kept me going was knowing that Jesus had forgiven me. That made me feel like a huge weight had been lifted from my shoulders and I daily reminded myself that I had a Father in heaven who loved me.

Eventually I found a job selling life assurance at Sanlam (one of the largest life assurance companies in South Africa), where two of my friends said to the regional manager that they would vouch for me. They persuaded him to give me a chance and I will forever be grateful to them for helping me to get that opportunity. If I had listed 50 jobs I would have been willing to do, being an assurance salesman would have been the very last one, but now I look back and see what a blessing it was. I had accrued so much debt that I was advised by friends who were attorneys to declare myself bankrupt. I couldn't do it. I had racked up the debts and I felt that I needed to pay them back. One attorney said, "You do know you'll be paying it back for the rest of your life, don't you?" I did, but it didn't change anything, it was something that I had to do. For days I went round on the bus to see the people I owed money to, apologising and promising to pay them back. Many were rightly angry with me for the way I had treated them. God may have forgiven me but I still had to live with the consequences of my actions and the world wasn't quick to forgive.

I worked hard—sometimes up to 16 hours a day—and I began to realise why God had given me the job he had. As I worked on commission only, life assurance was the one industry where you could almost write your own pay cheque. I used all the contacts that I had made during my sporting days and within three years I was one of the top 20 sales people for Sanlam in the country. Within five years I was able to start my own insurance brokerage business and, flying in the face of all the advice I received, I managed to pay back everything that I owed in just eight years. The harder I worked, the less time I had to drink so that eased my dependence on alcohol too.

A few years later God spoke to me whilst I was in a casino. He said I was to get out and never to put a foot back in a casino again. He set me free from the gambling addiction and I have never been back to a casino or to a racecourse again. What amazing grace!

I knew God had honoured the fact that I was trying to make amends for my mistakes and that I did it his way by paying back all my debt. He hadn't clicked his fingers and unravelled the mess of my life, but he took me by the hand and walked me through the difficult times. He never said that he would take us out of the valleys, but he did say that he would never leave or forsake us and that he would walk with us through those valleys.

When Jesus explained to Simon why he was being anointed by a sinful woman (Luke 7), he said that she had been forgiven so much that her love for him was great. I would say that I was the worst of sinners; I was in the gutter when I finally cried out to Jesus to save me. He welcomed me with open arms, never left my side through those tough times and all the terrible choices I had made. Where there is much forgiveness, there is great love. Like the sinful woman, I wanted to pour my life out at Jesus's feet in love and gratitude and follow him wherever he might lead.

Chapter 2

JOAN'S STORY

In all things God works for the good of those who love
him, who have been called according to his purpose.

Romans 8:28

I was born in Cape Town to a loving family, yet was welcomed into the world with howls of dismay. I turned out to be the youngest of three daughters rather than a longed-for son, who could play rugby for South Africa and follow my father into the family business.

Growing up, Jesus was hardly mentioned in our family, except as a swear word. Dad would refer to the church as "a bunch of hypocrites" and whatever he said was gospel for us. Yet many times as a child, I lay on the lawn outside of our house looking up at the stars, wondering if there was anyone out there, and what they would be like. I had such a sense of longing, yearning for something more.

Our parents sent us to a Church of England school, mainly so we would mix in the right circles and marry well. (I think my mother secretly hoped I would one day marry Prince Charles!) We attended chapel services, sang about Jesus and got confirmed, but I never quite understood or felt connected to this God that was spoken about. In the pictures I saw he was always so pale and thin, wearing a long white dress, or he was hanging on a cross, having suffered a gruesome death. Neither image made me want to know more about him or seemed realistic given he would probably have been a rugged, olive-skinned Israeli.

One of my earliest memories is of being given a box to collect coins for Dr. Barnardo's. All I knew was they were for poor children somewhere in England and—though I would occasionally take a knife to the coin slit to retrieve some of the funds for an ice cream—I always managed to hand in a full box in the end. It gave me a warm sense of accomplishment and though I didn't recognise it at the time, I think this was when the Holy Spirit first planted a seed deep inside of me to look out for some of the world's poorest children.

Sport was a big part of our family, and my dad taught us girls how to play golf. I played my first competition at the age of 10, went on to represent Western Province at the age of 17 and KwaZulu-Natal in my later years, while my sister, Felicity, played for South Africa. No matter how hard I tried, I was never able to beat her, probably because she would spend hours on the practice tee and I just wanted to pitch up and win. My school life was more focused on playing sport than the academics and as soon as I left school I continued to play golf and party. I joined a band as their female vocalist and when my dad heard me perform he told my mother, "Someone has to tell the child she can't sing"! My singing "career" lasted only a year, but I had a lot of fun and got to know some amazing people. For the next three years I trained and worked as a radiographer and continued to party but I felt like there was an emptiness inside me that I couldn't fill. Whatever I was doing I had the nagging thought, *There has to be more to life than this*.

APARTHEID

The 1950s and 60s were an interesting time to grow up in. South Africa claimed independence from the British Empire and entered into what would become a very dark time in the history of our country. We often ask ourselves how we could let the apartheid system turn us into a race who felt we were superior. There had always been a divide between the races, with "whites" and "non-whites", as we were called, going to different schools and not socialising together. When apartheid was declared law it seemed like just a formalisation of how things naturally were. The entire population was split into four categories: whites, blacks, Indians and coloureds.

It sounds strange now but it wasn't really discussed, and because so much media was banned—and TV didn't reach South Africa until the mid 70s—we only saw and heard the opinions the government wanted us to. All non-white people were issued with identity passes and our domestic help would have to show this pass to be allowed into the area where we lived. It wasn't legal to have a party where different races would mix but it would never have occurred to us to do that anyway. The buses and trains we rode on said "whites only", the beaches we visited said the same. Segregation was the world we knew.

I remember hearing about my older cousin, Mercia, a journalist, who went against the flow and was an activist against apartheid. I knew that people like Mercia were being followed by secret police trying to catch them in their rebellion. Although I accepted the status quo, her life caught my imagination. I can only look back and wish that I'd had the courage to stand up against the injustice of apartheid as she had done.

A NEW PERSPECTIVE

In 1970 I decided to leave South Africa and head off for an adventure in Europe, thinking this would be the thing that would satisfy the restlessness and occasional emptiness I felt inside. My father was relieved as it meant I left my long-haired musician boyfriend behind. He thought going abroad would help mature me and tame my "wild child" ways. I worked as a radiographer in hospitals and loved the new freedom I found and the fact I didn't have to worry about anyone but myself. I travelled for three months and then found a flat share in London with a great group of girls and stayed there for six months. Being part of a different culture opened up my eyes to the horrors of apartheid. For the first time I saw many races living alongside one another, integrated in a way I'd never imagined. I made up my mind to "divorce" my country and remain in the UK.

My one exception was to return for my sister Amanda's wedding, intending to go back for a few weeks and then head off again. But during this visit I met and fell in love with a professional golfer called Vincent Baker. We were married two years later. We lived in

Johannesburg for a while before heading for Durban, on the east coast, to be near the ocean. Vin was always passionate about fishing and I dreamt about having a home overlooking the ocean. We travelled a lot on the South African and European golf tours and I alternated between being the caddie and working as a radiographer, at home and abroad, to subsidise our income. Travelling with a group of players and their wives so frequently meant we became like a large extended family and we shared many special times on our trips. We didn't take life too seriously and partied hard.

We had two children, Grant and Kate, and Vin continued to travel on the golf tours, which often meant he was away for months at a time. It took its toll on us as a family. There were no mobile phones, no Skype or text messages, only letters and occasionally a phone call. These times of separation were long and painful, resulting in my life feeling like a series of highs and lows.

I had help with the children in the form of Nora, the nanny and domestic worker who lived with us. Nora's two children spent many holidays playing with Grant and Kate in our back garden, but they weren't allowed to go out with us. They couldn't visit the same beaches as us or sit in the same restaurant to have a milkshake. Despite having my eyes opened on my travels I had quickly settled back into a system that was unjust and cruel. Like so many white South Africans, I accepted the status quo of apartheid. Things were good for us and all I cared about was myself, my family and my friends. Now I look back with such regret that, though we loved and accepted Nora and her children as part of our family, we accepted it as the norm that they weren't treated as our equals.

A NEW BUSINESS VENTURE

Money was often tight, as we were largely reliant on Vin's golf swing to pay our bills, so I continued to work and we looked for other business opportunities. When I was with Vin and the rest of the golfers we would often talk about the lack of decent golf clothing. We joined up with South African golf pros Dale Hayes, Simon Hobday and Peter Matkovich, to produce a range of golf wear which we called Rhythm. We didn't really know what we were doing, but we had great fun along the way.

Rhythm was eventually sold, and Vin and I went on to buy a clothing factory and manufactured a range of ladies' golf and tennis wear under the Circuit Sportswear label. We knew a golf pro who had connections with a clothing distribution company in the UK so I saved up to go to England in the early 80s to try and sell our range there. I didn't know the protocol for these types of sales and, having decided I wanted our range in Harrods, I went straight to the golf pro who ran the golf shop there. I showed him pictures and told him the African colours in our range would make a welcome change for customers from the dull tartans and browns he had on display. Thankfully he wasn't put off by my cheek and he loved the idea. He sent me to the buyer who promptly told me to come back six months later as they had already finished their buying for that season. I didn't want to tell him that I had already spent all the money we had on me getting there and there was no way I could come over again, so I went back to the pro. He had obviously been at Harrods for many years and clearly was used to getting what he wanted so he called the buyer and an hour later I walked out of the shop with an order placed.

WHEN GRACE SHOWED UP

Life for our entire family changed the day my sister Felicity's three-year-old daughter, Leigh, was diagnosed with an inoperable brain tumour. She had experienced a number of seizures. Up until then, if we had a problem our dad was always able to fix it. Now the doctors said they couldn't do anything and we were heartbroken and desperate. Felicity and a friend were speaking on the phone and decided that if there was a God out there they should ask him for help. Neither of them were believers, but they agreed each one would go to their respective bathrooms and pray. We aren't sure to this day why they thought the bathroom was a good choice!

Felicity ended up going to a church with her neighbour, announcing a few weeks later that she was now "born again". We thought she'd joined a cult. A couple of months later she announced that this God she had met was healing Leigh. Our alarm bells went off and we proceeded to tell her that people don't just get healed. To our complete amazement and joy the next test showed that the tumour was completely gone! The doctors had no logical explanation and as a family we were faced with the reality that this Jesus Felicity had spoken of was clearly real.

One by one our family members accepted Jesus as Lord and Saviour but I was hesitant. I didn't want to give up my lifestyle of revelry, consuming copious amounts of alcohol and spending many hours in the golf club pub. Felicity constantly reminded me I wasn't going to heaven which infuriated me in her presence but when I was alone the thought niggled away at me.

One Sunday in November 1981 I was lying in bed with my usual weekend hangover when my daughter, Kate, came into my room and asked why she had to go to Sunday school with her aunt when I could take her. Feeling guilty I agreed to go only to find myself in a church with a group of strange people singing their hearts out, waving their hands in the air and smiling away. They completely freaked me out. After the singing the preacher got up wearing an open neck shirt and cracking jokes from the pulpit. I was amazed I could actually understand what he was talking about, having expected it to be a load of religious mumbo jumbo. At the end of his sermon he asked if there were any of us who felt we weren't going to heaven. I knew that was me (and if I hadn't Felicity's elbow nudging me in the ribs would have reminded me). Thinking I should be honest in church, I raised my hand. To my horror he told us to come forward but I wouldn't budge. He added that he knew which of us had put our hands up and appeared to be looking straight at me. Terrified, I shot out of the pew just in case he decided to drag me up.

As I walked up the aisle I began to sob. I had no idea why and kept telling myself to stop but to no avail. By the time I reached the front with the few others who dared to venture forward, I was making so much noise I couldn't hear a word the pastor said. They eventually ushered me into a little side room to get rid of me and a lady asked me if I knew what I had done. Between sobs I told her that I didn't have a clue; all I knew was I wasn't going to heaven. She asked if I wanted to receive Jesus and I said, "Whatever it takes, lady."

I thought that was the end of it and I could go back to my life, ticket to heaven now in my back pocket, but then I noticed little things starting to happen. Every time I blasphemed, I felt uncomfortable. I felt guilty every time I had too much to drink. I began to enjoy hearing all the Bible stories that Felicity was keen to tell me at every opportunity. I told all my friends that it was easy to get into heaven; all you had to do was say a prayer inviting Jesus into your heart. Most thought I had lost my mind and some even ran away.

Poor Vin received the brunt of this outpouring as I tried to get him to book his place in heaven, convinced it was my responsibility to get him saved. He said that if God was so powerful then he must reveal himself to him. I was so frustrated that he wouldn't listen to me! I spent the following years doing the splits with one foot in God's kingdom and the other in the world. I was like a sponge, soaking up all that I was learning in the many Bible studies Felicity was taking me to and also soaking up too much alcohol! I may not have been the best witness for Christ, repeating what I was learning about him in between whiskies.

When Felicity first became a Christian, dad used to refer to her as "the bishop". When challenged he would say he was ready to meet his Maker. We prayed many prayers for him, especially that he would not die by surprise and that he would have an opportunity to recognise that you can live without Jesus, but you definitely don't want to die without him. When he was diagnosed with cancer at the age of 76, and the doctors said there was nothing more they could do, he wasn't so sure he was ready to meet his Maker after all, and it was in those last days that Felicity was able to lead him to the Lord.

On the advice of a wise minister, I gave up trying to "convert" my long-suffering husband and prayed for him instead. One day he came back from a golf tournament and announced he had found the Lord on the golf course. He described how, whilst walking down the 16th fairway, he said out loud to God, "I really do believe in you." The following hole, he hit his drive in deep grass. He could barely see the ball and it was almost impossible to make contact between it and the club. In front of him was thick bush and a large tree with a small gap. He needed two pars to finish the round and qualify for the final two rounds. He swung the club towards where he thought the ball was and it came out of the grass perfectly, went through the tiny gap in the tree and landed on the green. He knew there was no way he could have made that shot himself and it must have been God's help (which of course sounded ludicrous but was very real to him).

In answer to my many prayers Jesus had met my husband right where he was at. But, like me, he was torn between two worlds. He never wanted to come to church or read a Bible but he would tell his friends, and especially his fellow golf pros, how he had "found the Man" and that if he died he was going to heaven. They laughed him off and told him to have another drink.

WHEN LIFE STOPPED

As a keen fisherman Vin would often head out to the Tongaat river mouth, a 15-minute drive from our home on the north coast of Durban. In July 1990 he left the clothing factory one Thursday afternoon to go fishing and was due to meet me at my sister's house for dinner that evening with my mother. My father had died six months previously and our family were still recovering from the loss. Vin hadn't arrived by the time the food was ready so we started to eat and thought he would join us. Soon it was time to go home and he'd neither turned up nor phoned to tell us where he was. There were no mobiles so I couldn't call him but when I got home I tried calling his friend Ian, imagining I'd find him there. Ian hadn't heard from him, and I knew then something was wrong. Going to bed feeling sick I hoped he would show up with an excuse about how he'd been out drinking and lost track of time.

When there was still no sign of him in the morning I called the police. They said they wouldn't start looking until he'd been gone 24 hours. Not wanting to sit around and wait, I rallied a group of friends and we started to search the area around the Tongaat river mouth. We combed every bit of land, and even dredged the river in case he had drowned, but we found nothing.

I made a pamphlet bearing Vin's photo and a picture of the car he'd been in, offering a reward for any information, and we dropped them all around the surrounding areas using a small aeroplane. Life for me, Grant and Kate (who were 17 and 13) had stopped. For five days we searched for him. Thanks to Vin's golfing career we received a lot of press coverage, which helped widen our search, but no one had seen him. Despair enveloped us like a black cloud with tinges of hope that maybe he would still walk through the front door. I believed in miracles and kept praying for one.

We received calls from spiritualists and mediums offering to tell us where he was but I told them we were trusting in Jesus. Five days after Vin had gone missing we were completely exhausted and at the end of ourselves. We were incredibly vulnerable and were absolutely desperate to know where he was. That night Vin's family took a call from one of the detectives who said if we gave him an article of his clothing they could help find him. This, I knew, was an offer to use a witchdoctor or a sangoma.[1]

---

1   A spiritualist.

The family were sorely tempted, as we would have done almost anything to know what had happened. I told them they needed to trust me and that we couldn't use both the kingdom of light and the kingdom of darkness. I knew that God had heard our prayers and even though I couldn't bear the thought of it I believed with all my heart that even if we never found him, God would have a reason for that and we had to trust him.

As soon as I called the detective back and told him our decision, the breakthrough call came. The call we had all been waiting for and dreading. Someone had seen the Kombi[2] Vin had been driving abandoned in a local township. The next morning the police went in, found the vehicle and three young teenagers, who confessed they had hijacked Vin's car and when he fought back had stabbed and killed him. They took the police to where they had left his body, deep in the sugar cane not far from the river mouth where he had been fishing. We thought we had prepared to hear the worst during those days of waiting but nothing can ever really prepare you to hear that someone you love has been so cruelly and viciously taken from you. It felt like our world had ended.

I knew my Father in heaven was with me, but there were times when I felt like I was going into a black pit of despair. I was still reeling from my dad's death and now I had been widowed at the age of 40. I'd lost the two most important men in my life in just six months. All I could do was hang on to the hem of Jesus's garment; I didn't dare let go. I tried to make a deal with God, telling him that I didn't want to be in this world anymore. The life I had

---

2   A seven-seater van.

known and loved was over for good and there was little left for me to live for. I loved my children with all my heart but I couldn't see how I could keep going with the weight of this excruciating pain bearing down on me day after day. Through the fog of my grief I asked God to take me home to be with him as soon as they didn't need me anymore.

THE KEYS TO HEALING

As I stumbled through those painful days, weeks and months that followed, God spoke to me very clearly about the keys that would help me keep going and find life again:

• *Forgive*

Just a few hours after hearing the news of Vin's murder I had been asked by a reporter if I would forgive the young people who had taken his life. My immediate response was to say yes, but doing it was another matter altogether. I realised that forgiving the three young guys had nothing to do with my emotions but was an act of my will and I had to choose it in order to be obedient to God's Word. It wasn't about whether I thought they were worthy of forgiveness, or even if they asked for it; God wanted me to forgive them so that I could be free from the bitterness and hatred that would have eaten me up otherwise. God reminded me that judgement and vengeance must be left to him and not taken into our own hands.

I also had to forgive Vin for leaving me; rationally I knew it wasn't his fault but I was so angry that he had fought back and kept thinking if he had just given them the car he would still be with us.

• *Self-Pity Is a Sin*

When I heard God say this I put up a fight. I wanted to feel sorry for myself and thought I had the absolute right to. But as I trusted him and began to let go of my self-pity I realised this wasn't about denying my feelings and pretending I was OK with what had happened, it was about not sinking into a mindset of "poor me". Self-pity would lead me further into a pit of depression and I had to choose as an act of my will to resist it every time it came knocking on my door and before it brought all of its "friends" with it.

• *Give Thanks*

This flummoxed me too. My first thought was, *God, what have I got to be thankful for?* I felt like my life was done; my whole future had been ripped away. But as I pondered on this I realised God was showing me how to overcome the pain that was so overwhelming. Thanksgiving isn't an emotional response for when life is going well, but an act of the will that we must choose if we want to be obedient to him. So I wilfully began to give thanks. I thanked God for answering my prayers that Vin would be found. I thanked him that he had revealed himself to Vin 18 months before he died, forgiving him his sins, and that my husband was now in heaven with Jesus. I thanked him for our two children. I thanked him that we still had a roof over our heads and food on the table. I kept on and on, thanking him for every little thing I could think of, and as I did so I felt the oppressive heaviness of my grief begin to lift.

• *Praise Me*

My immediate response was, *Wow, Lord, how can you expect me to praise you right now?* It was the last thing that I felt like doing, but the thought persisted and I chose to do it once again by an act of will. At first there was no feeling, but slowly the deadness I felt inside began to stir to life again. I knew this wasn't about an egotistical God demanding my gratitude and praise with no compassion for the trauma I was facing, but a loving Father leading me down the road of recovery and total healing. I've learned that God is by far the best psychologist you can have, and he is available day and night, for free!

I have shared these four keys that God gave me with many people over the years who have lost loved ones, or are dealing with another type of grief and pain. They seem counter-intuitive at first but they bring such incredible freedom and healing. I also realised that all the Bible studies I had attended and the sermons I had heard helped me to stand firm in my faith. During this dark time Satan wanted me to embrace bitterness, unforgiveness, self-pity and depression, to lose my faith and turn my back on God. Instead the Word of God kicked into gear and became a weapon for me to use. No wonder God wants us to know him and his Word so when life's trials and tribulations come we are able to stand firm in him.

THE COURT CASE

A year later we had to face the hurdle of the court case. The three young men had pleaded not guilty and I was a witness with regard to identifying Vin's personal items that were found in their possession. I didn't want to have to come face to face with his killers and asked God to take this "cup" from me whilst saying if he needed me to go through that as part of my journey of total restoration, then so be it. I also prayed there would be no journalists, though there had been keen media interest in the case. Felicity and I arrived at the courthouse on the Friday morning and my heart sank when I saw a photographer already waiting at the steps. I took a deep breath, prayed and walked past him. It was like we were invisible. He looked right through us and made no move to take a picture or talk to us.

Then came the second answer to prayer: the accused had changed their pleas to guilty and I didn't need to testify. The air around me felt thick with God's grace. The young men were sentenced to seven years in a rehabilitation centre and I knew God was saying to me that this process had nothing to do with me and I had to leave them in his hands. I'd lost my husband and the future I thought was ahead of me, but Vin was in heaven with his Lord, and God was leading me into the next season he had planned and purposed for my life. I continued to run our factory and walk with my children on the journey of recovery. My sisters were very worried I would end up in the bottom of a bottle again, and maybe God was too, because he brought Tich into my life very quickly.

Chapter 3

OUT OF THE ASHES

Bestow on them a crown of beauty instead of ashes, the oil of joy instead of mourning, and a garment of praise instead of a spirit of despair.

Isaiah 61:3

Joan

Tich and I knew each other from being in the same sporting circles, and after he heard about Vin's death he offered his help with my insurances. People say, "Beware the insurance salesman." Well, I didn't! A few months later Tich took me out for tea and said that God had told him to look after me and my children. I told him he was mad! God had definitely not told me anything of the sort and I told him about my deal with God that he would take me home as soon as my children didn't need me anymore. Even having a conversation like that with Tich felt like I was betraying Vin. I had made up my mind that I was never going to love again. The loss of a loved one was just too painful and I thought that part of my life was over.

In the following months Tich phoned regularly to see how we were doing. The calls started to come every day and it felt too much; I asked God to stop Tich from calling me because I felt like I was being unfaithful. The calls stopped and, typically, I missed them straight away. I took Kate and Grant on a skiing trip with my sister's family and while I was away I realised my feelings for Tich were stronger than friendship. I was missing his company and had begun to think about how cute he was. We both realised that we had fallen in love. It was a complete shock to me that I could love again and I cancelled my deal with God to go home.

Neither of us likes to wait around when we know what we want so we decided to get married as soon as my children were ready. We put our respective houses on the market, thinking it would take at least six months to sell them. Tich's sold within a week and mine at the first showing! My brother-in-law, who was a property developer, called me to say he had a house he thought we might like and when we saw it we instantly fell in love with it. It was our dream home with five bedrooms and was just across the road from the beach with stunning views over the Indian Ocean. We bought it immediately and moved in; I convinced myself that it was OK to live together because we planned to get married as soon as Grant and Kate were ready.

Tich

Although I had been a Christian for a few years, I wasn't part of a church and I didn't read my Bible. I had a rough idea that living together before marriage wasn't right but I didn't think it was a big deal. Then a few months after we moved in, I woke up with a strong conviction that what we were doing was wrong. I turned to Joan and said, "I have to get out of here." She thought I had gone mad but I knew we couldn't live together until we were married. We decided to get married that same week in our living room. I told Joan to phone her guy at church and to tell him we could get married on Friday afternoon or Saturday morning. The Saturday afternoon was out as there was a big rugby match between the Sharks and the Bulls!

My children were away at boarding school and Joan's daughter, Kate, didn't want any part of the wedding as she was still grieving her dad's death. Grant agreed to give his mother away and at the last minute his friends arrived to pick him up for an evening out. He told them to wait in his room; he wouldn't be long, he just had to give his mother away.

MARRIED LIFE BEGINS

Joan

Second marriages, we soon discovered, aren't wedded bliss. In fact, all hell broke loose in our home as we brought two families together, with Grant and Kate still struggling with the loss of their father and feeling the natural betrayal of us moving on with our lives. Tich, having lived the life of a bachelor for five years, suddenly found himself with a new wife, two teenage stepchildren and two Doberman dogs.

On top of that I developed a cyst the size of an avocado which burst, filling my body with poison, and I needed an emergency operation which left me bedridden for three months. Kate, at the age of 14, had mastered the teenage art of expressing how she felt without saying a word. When I got back from the hospital, the tension in the home was so tangible that my insides went into a spasm and I had to return to the hospital. They gave me morphine for the pain and I lay in a state of euphoria for two days. I begged them to keep me on morphine, preferably for a few years, but instead they sent me back home.

Amazingly the four children got along well together from the start and Julie and Greg accepted me straight away. Kate and Grant continued to struggle to accept Tich, and he wasn't sure how to handle them either as he'd never lived full-time with teenagers before, let alone stepchildren. He often hid in our bedroom, seeking refuge from his new family. When emotions were running high and we least felt like it we would sit at the end of our bed and pray together. We often had to force the words out through gritted teeth, asking God to help us even though we were both bristling with irritation at each other.

As in most second marriages, we mostly disagreed about how to handle the children. Vin and I had always disciplined our children strictly but when he died I just wanted to make life as easy as possible for Kate and Grant so I completely relaxed the rules. It was especially hard for Tich as he didn't want to step in and try and take the place of their father but wanted to be a friend and support them. I felt guilty for looking like I'd moved on from Vin's death though I was in fact still grieving. Tich was amazingly patient and kind and would hold me as I wept and wept. It was a very odd time to be a newlywed whilst still grieving the loss of my first husband.

It was a year after our wedding that we had a proper reception in our home for our families and friends. It was a wonderful occasion, as our children were all ready to celebrate our marriage and our family becoming one. Many people encounter difficulties bringing two families together and we learnt that God doesn't take away our problems but he does promise to walk through the valley times with us. Our relationship had started under unusual circumstances but God was working all things together for good. Grace was turning our mourning into dancing again. We had a beautiful home by the ocean, a steady income, and most importantly each other.

PART II
Raised

Chapter 4

A GOD WHO HEALS

So if the Son sets you free, you will be free indeed.

John 8:36

Tich

Though I had been a Christian for a number of years and was now making a fresh start at married life, I was still stuck in many of my old ways, particularly when I was around people from my sporting days. I had started attending church with Joan and I knew my Father in heaven loved me but there was little outward evidence to suggest I was a Christian. I was the best undercover agent that Jesus ever had because only Jesus, Peter Pollock, Joan and I knew I had given my life to him!

A year after our wedding I returned to my old school in Johannesburg for the annual cricket game that many of the alumni took part in, playing against the school's first team. After the game we got together over a few drinks as we hadn't seen one another for many years. The party went on into the early hours of the following morning. Shortly after I had to drive back home as Joan and I were due to play golf with her sister and brother-in-law. I had a terrible hangover and I cried out to God, "This can't be your plan for my life. I can't stop drinking. I need you to take the taste for alcohol away."

I had tried to stop many times in my own strength with no success. I felt completely powerless against the pull of alcohol that had dominated my life for so long but after praying that prayer in the car I can honestly say that, over 20 years later, I have never desired another drop. There was a brief moment of temptation the following Christmas when I was offered a glass of champagne which I resisted and that was the last time I thought about saying yes.

It wasn't an easy road; for many years I was mocked and teased in the pub after golf. My friends couldn't believe I had stopped drinking and thought it was just a passing phase. They didn't understand it was a miraculous healing that changed my life forever. I began to understand in a new way that God wants the best for us and how powerful it is to pray in the name of Jesus. The local AA invited me to speak at one of their meetings and when I shared that I was no longer an alcoholic as Jesus had miraculously healed me, they said I was confusing people and didn't invite me back. They didn't understand that when Jesus sets you free you are free indeed. I know as long as Jesus is Lord of my life I will never touch another drop of alcohol. God has removed the three things that once crippled my life: alcohol, gambling and womanising. In my own strength I was unable to overcome these things, but in Christ Jesus all things are possible.

FROM DEATH TO LIFE

It was a few years later that Gary Verne contacted me. He was a well-known South African jockey who had become one of my closest friends when I was spending most of my days at the races. We had partied a lot together and become very close, but he had left Durban to ride in Cape Town and we'd lost touch. He called me out of the blue and asked me to come and meet him but I said no. I was really frank with him and said that my drinking and gambling days were behind me and I didn't think it would be a good idea to see him.

Over the next few weeks when I was praying, Gary kept coming into my mind and I realised it was the Holy Spirit prompting me to go and see him. He and his wife, Sue, lived on a smallholding outside Pietermaritzburg near where my children were at boarding school, so I said I'd visit when I picked them up at the end of term. When I arrived it was clear they had fallen on hard times; many young jockeys in those days had an "easy come, easy go" philosophy when it came to money. Gary also looked thin and frail and told me he'd contracted hepatitis B whilst riding in Mauritius.

Gary had seen me at my worst and couldn't believe how different I was. He was keen to know why my life had changed so much. I told him I'd given my life to Jesus and that he had delivered me from my addictions and that I'd been able to start my own insurance brokerage. Gary knew that I couldn't have made these changes on my own and I was pretty sure he wanted to give his life to the Lord having seen what God had done for me. I should have offered to pray with him but I didn't have the courage or faith as I had never prayed with anyone before.

He went on to tell me he was under pressure from the banks, so we phoned them to make a plan for him to pay back what he owed and tried to get a disability claim from the Jockeys' Provident Fund as the hepatitis B had prevented him from having a full riding schedule. The life assurance company told us they couldn't help as they only covered jockeys for accidental disability and not disability through illness. I left with a heavy heart. I kept replaying the conversation we'd had and felt terrible that I hadn't told him more about Jesus and given him an opportunity to become a Christian.

A month later Sue phoned to say that Gary's hepatitis B had led to him contracting the flu and his temperature was spiking and plummeting causing a seizure. After he recovered from the seizure he asked for me to come and see him and I said I would go the following day as the hospital was 90 kilometres away. Before I could set off I received a phone call saying he'd had another seizure that had lasted for three hours and was now in a coma and on a life support machine. The doctors said there was no chance of him recovering; the best case scenario was him being in a vegetative state.

I was devastated. I knew I should have prayed with him and felt terrible that he was dying without having met with Jesus. I was still young in my faith and thought I had to get to Jesus through Peter Pollock, so I called and asked him what I should do. Peter always pointed me to Jesus and told me to ask God myself, so I prayed and felt God wanted me to go to the hospital and pray for Gary. I had never done that in my life so I phoned Joan and she said she would come with me. I drove there feeling like a complete failure for not sharing Jesus when I had the opportunity.

When we arrived we were told Gary had been declared brain dead and that the doctors were waiting to turn off his life support. We went straight to the ICU and pleaded to be let in. As we entered the room we saw that Gary was as white as the sheets he was lying under. The room was quiet except for the ticking of the life support machine. I said to God, "I don't know what I'm doing here but you've told me to come so I pray you would heal Gary by the power of your Holy Spirit. Please bring him back because I know he wanted to give his life to you. Give him the opportunity to do that and then you can take him home." Joan sat beside me making funny noises and I thought she'd gone mad because I'd never heard anyone praying in tongues before. We eventually left the room with heavy hearts after saying our last goodbyes.

We met Sue and Gary's mum, Dolly, in the waiting room and prayed with them that God would help them prepare for his death. I phoned the hospital that night and they reported there had been no change and they were waiting for the family to give them permission to turn off his life support. The very next day Sue called. Gary had come out of his coma! He couldn't speak because he still had a tube in his throat to help him breathe but he was able to write a note to ask why he was in hospital. We were stunned. There was no brain damage. God had answered our prayers and given Gary a second chance!

Gary made a full recovery that none of the doctors could comprehend. Then about three months later Sue called me on a Sunday evening and from the excitement in her voice I thought they must have won the jackpot and had all of their money problems solved as well as the healing. Instead her words came out in a rush, "Things have never been worse. The bank have repossessed our cars and the smallholding but we went to the Baptist church to get food for our children and there was a service and they asked if anyone wanted to give their life to Jesus. I went forward! When I looked back, Gary was right behind me! We both gave our lives to Jesus!"

Two days later I received a fax saying that the underwriters of the Jockeys' Provident Fund had reconsidered Gary's case (even though we hadn't asked them to) and they paid out a sum which in today's money would be around R3.5 million (£170,000/$240,000). It was an astounding turnaround that we knew God had orchestrated.

A year later Gary went fishing at a dam near his home with his stepson Aaron and a friend of his. They hired a boat but a propeller got caught in the reeds and they had no oar. They weren't far from the shore so Aaron and his friend jumped into the water to swim to get help. It was a winter's day and the water was very cold so they started to get numb. Fearing they were drowning they cried out to Gary who immediately jumped in to push them to safety. When they looked back Gary had disappeared under the water. His body wasn't found till five days later. God had given Gary a second chance to get his life right and exactly a year after he had recovered from the coma, Jesus took him home to be with him. I will be eternally grateful to my Father for hearing my cry that Gary wouldn't die without receiving eternal life from Jesus.

I had the privilege of speaking at Gary's funeral and was able to share this testimony on Gary's behalf. The church was packed that day with many from the racing fraternity and others who had known and loved Gary, and many lives were touched and changed. I was reminded again that you can choose to live without Jesus but you don't want to die without him. That day I declared to God, "Take my life, Lord, and do what you will with it." He gave his all for us and all he wants is all of us.

Chapter 5

A BIG VISION AND SMALL BEGINNINGS

*Religion that God our Father accepts as pure and faultless
is this: to look after orphans and widows in their distress
and to keep oneself from being polluted by the world.*

James 1:27

Tich

Though I'd long since stopped playing sport professionally, I still enjoyed a bit of healthy competition, so I started playing competitive golf. I played every weekend and often during the week, practising most evenings after work. I always had a special relationship with the caddies at the golf club. Many of them were wayward guys who came from very poor communities. They had little education and would often steal from the bags they were supposed to be looking after. They also had a wonderful sense of humour and they appreciated being treated as equals as this wasn't the norm. We became real friends to the point that one of them asked to come to church with me.

To my surprise I felt God say no. Instead he said to take the church to them. I contacted a pastor Joan knew called Derrick Gumede and said, "If I pick you up at 6 a.m. will you come with me to spend time with the caddies?" He agreed, and so we would go every Tuesday and Friday to hang out at the caddie shack (the canteen where the caddies would wait to get a bag to carry). In the beginning only two caddies joined us but I believe God was testing our hearts and asking us if we were prepared to make the effort for just two people. Everything starts with small beginnings and gradually others started to join until we had 40–50 guys there each week. I would get up at 5 a.m. and make peanut butter and jam sandwiches for the guys, and then Derrick and I would head to the caddie shack to share the gospel.

Many of the caddies gave their lives to Jesus and it was incredible to see how their lives changed. Even the golf club members noticed as fewer things were getting stolen and they could see the changes in the lives of these guys. They began to ask questions and the caddies were able to minister to the golfers as they shared their testimonies of how Jesus was changing them. A special story that touched my heart is when one of the golfers told me that he blasphemed after missing a short putt and his caddie asked him to stop using the name of Jesus as a swear word. The golfer asked him what had happened to him and he said that Pastor Tich was teaching them about Jesus who was now Lord of his life.

We loved these changes but of course they, like us all, were still works in progress. A classic example of this was when one of the caddies stole R600 (£30/$40) out of the bag he was carrying. I was summoned to the club by the manager who had a very irate golfer with him who happened to be a policeman. I was asked to investigate what had happened to the money and I found out who was carrying the bag, asking the caddie why he had stolen the money. I had taught them they must never take what is not theirs, whether it was two cents or R1,000. I told the caddie that this golfer was a policeman who was threatening to shoot him. His reply was, "Eish, Pastor Tich, if I had known he was a policeman I wouldn't have stolen the money."

It was another opportunity to minister through life lessons. The Word of God tells us to go and make disciples and this can often be a long and slow process where you take two steps forward and one step back. We are also reminded that God never promised an easy ride; in fact, he says in this life we *will* have trouble.

I wanted to do more to help so I asked myself, what do the caddies need the most? They earned very little money and what they had seemed to go on food and transport, so I thought if I could help with one of those, they would have more money to live on. I decided to buy a 40-seater air-conditioned bus. It cost me R100,000 (£5,000/$7,000) and one of the caddies told me he had a licence to drive it. (As it turned out he couldn't drive a bike, let alone a bus!)

The first morning I waited for them at the club and heard the loud music from a great distance as the bus came towards me, but when it parked, only three people were on board. The rest of the guys had decided they didn't want to get up so early and asked for the bus to come back later! It was a disaster and a waste of money in many ways but I'm convinced that God doesn't mind mistakes; he just wants to see our hearts. Three accidents and a burnt out engine later we sold the bus and notched up the experience as another lesson learnt.

Fear of failure is not an option. It paralyses and causes us to do nothing, which is far worse in his eyes. I had jumped in head first, thinking it was a good idea, but it was clearly not God's idea. (One of my mentors once said that a "good" idea has one too many "o"s in it!) However, it was the starting point for me to look to the needs of others and, as God always works all things together for good, it was also a catalyst for others to begin to minister to caddies around Durban, telling them about Jesus and teaching them a new way of life. Many lives have been touched and changed because Christians reached out in love. Poverty is incredibly tough and the way of life they knew was to steal and cheat to get what they needed. We needed to help them see there was a different way of doing things.

Joan

One of the caddies was desperately sick with the AIDS virus to the point he couldn't carry a bag. I was walking into church one morning when he came in looking for Tich. I took one look at him and thought he was about to die. He was so thin—skeletal in fact—and I didn't know how he was even managing to walk. Derrick and I took him into the chapel to pray for him, sitting either side of him and repeatedly saying, "Don't be afraid. You've given your life to Jesus." I reassured him that as soon as he died he would be with Jesus and that he had nothing to fear.

We prayed like this for a while and then I added on, almost as an afterthought, "The Bible also says we can pray for healing." I wanted to be obedient to God's Word even though I had no faith he would get healed. So I put my hand on his shoulder, not sure if he'd even live to the end of my prayer, and asked Jesus to heal him. After we prayed he shuffled out of the church looking just as bad as when he came in.

A week or so later I asked Derrick if he'd taken his funeral. "What funeral?" he replied. "He's back on the golf course caddying again!" God clearly didn't need me to have faith for healing in order for him to do it and that guy became a great evangelist, testifying and ministering to other caddies and his community, eventually taking over from Tich and Derrick. I realised that day that God doesn't really need us but chooses to work through us. All we have to do is be obedient to his Word. What a privilege that he wants to partner with us to make a difference in the lives of others.

A SURPRISING VISION

Tich

That's where my ministry started—reaching out to the caddies at golf clubs. They were the ones, besides the golfers, who came across my path every week. I'd never had anything to do with people living in poverty before and I had no heart to serve them. It had never entered my mind. As a sportsman you're trained to think about your own performance and I was very self-centred, with little concern for the needs of others.

Then I went on a men's weekend with Peter Pollock in Nelspruit, on the border of the Kruger National Park, where he was speaking. He flew back and I had an eight-hour drive to get back to Durban. I'd been inspired by the teaching of the Word that weekend and I began to worship as I drove. For the next two and a half hours I prayed in tongues, not knowing what I was saying. I had never done that before and it took me completely by surprise. I then screamed at the Lord, "Surely there's more to life than this; please speak to me." For the next six hours I listened. (Which in itself was a miracle!)

God showed me the most beautiful bougainvillea flower, blossoming in the middle of a dry area and said, "That is what the church should be like." He said I must build a village for orphaned and vulnerable children and create an environment where they would come to know him as their Father. As I drove past communities on hilltops he said that's what it would look like. He told me to create jobs for rural communities that would help them sustain their families and said that leaders in the government would come and see why it worked, and we would be able to point them to the cross.

The vision was crystal clear but that didn't make it any less ludicrous. I'd never even set foot in a rural community before, and the only contact I'd had with the poor was ministering to the caddies. I was too embarrassed to tell anyone except Joan because the whole thing sounded so crazy. How on earth could we do it, and why would leaders of the government ever come and see something we were doing? We didn't even know anyone in government!

Joan thought I'd lost my mind and couldn't wrap her head around what I was saying as it was so completely out of the blue. Nothing in our past had led us to thinking this was in our future. We didn't even feel like we'd been very good parents to our own children, let alone taking responsibility for many more. And we had no idea what job creation had to do with looking after orphans. But I drew her a picture of what God had shown me with a few houses, a long winding road that went up a hill and past crops, a sports field, a school, a church and a huge cross that could be seen for miles around.

Tich and Joan

The vision blew us away and our first thought was that if we were going to build a village, we needed to find some land, start a building company and get building. We connected with the local government at city hall and gave them a very rough plan of what we wanted to do. They told us it was a wonderful idea but they had no interest in getting involved. In the meantime, we'd started a building business, buying a half-built house and aiming to complete it and sell it on to make money to start the village. When it was ready no one was interested in buying it and we realised we had no idea what we were doing! We put it up for auction and by God's grace we managed to get back the money we'd invested. More importantly, though, all of the workers we employed through the business gave their lives to Jesus. It might not have been successful in the world's eyes, but it was prosperous in the eyes of God.

Though we laughed about it, the situation only confirmed that we had no clue what we were doing. We had jumped in without waiting for God to speak and direct us about his timing. We've learned that this is often the way; you get a vision and get excited by it but trusting in God means trusting him for the timing too. We felt it was a bit like Abraham jumping ahead and having Ishmael after God told him he would have a son, rather than waiting and trusting for Sarah to get pregnant with Isaac. We always felt God didn't mind our mistakes because he knew our hearts were in the right place. We often visualise Christians being like ships in the harbour (the church). When we set sail out of the safety and calm of the harbour, untying ourselves from the world's system, and going out into the ocean, where it is rough and unpredictable, and not knowing where we are going, we may go in the wrong direction but God is able to move the rudder and steer us along the right path. If we stay safely in the harbour, there's not much he can do.

God was stirring us and we knew there had to be more to this Christian life than just reading the Word and attending church on Sundays and cell groups during the week. James 1:27 says, "Religion that God our Father accepts as pure and faultless is this: to look after orphans and widows in their distress." In fact, God's Word talks about the poor over 2,535 times; if we don't listen to his call to look after the widow, the orphan, the destitute and the lost, we are leaving a huge hole in our gospel. We began to realise that as believers we *are* the church and we don't just know the answer to many of the problems in the world, we *are* the answer. God only has one plan and that is the local church. He doesn't have plan B and he is waiting for us to hear his heartbeat for those in need.

We knew God wanted so much more for us and from us. We needed to put his Word into action; it was time to live it. We were beginning to realise this journey with Jesus was not about being religious (in fact he hated religion) but about being his hands and feet, following in his footsteps, as his disciples did. They were just an ordinary group of people, like us, working for a living, who said yes to Jesus. They left the harbour and, once they received the power of the Holy Spirit, they changed the world, one person at a time. Nothing was easy about their walk of faith and obedience, but they never wavered, even unto death. They had found the pearl of great price … and nothing else compared. Like the early disciples, we didn't know where we were going but we knew that he knew and that he would direct us. We just had to trust that his grace would be sufficient.

Chapter 6

TRAINING GROUND

We make a living by what we get. We make a life by what we give.

Sir Winston Churchill

Joan

After Tich's vision and the failure of the building business, we got distracted by life and the idea of the village went onto the back burner. Our four kids were leaving home, heading off to university and overseas travels, and Tich was working hard to pay all the bills. I was itching to get back into business and managed to persuade him to let me turn our home into a guest house to provide some extra income. Guests came from all over the world, and we even had the president of Zimbabwe come and stay which was an interesting experience! It was a learning process for us both to be open with our home and to share it with strangers; something that was useful training for what was to come.

Two ladies who worked for us at the guest house kept telling me about the starving children in the township where they lived, called Amaoti. I asked where that was and they said it was some 20 kilometres over the hill from where we lived. It was so close but I'd never been there or even heard of it. In fact, I'd never been into any township. We later discovered that it is one of the biggest informal settlements in KwaZulu-Natal with over 100,000 residents. They started telling me that many gangs operated from there, and said there were many children in Amaoti who were starving and neglected, being abused, often living on the streets, knocking on strangers' doors and asking for food. I was shocked that this was just up the road from our beautiful beach house and it played on my mind as I wondered if there was anything I could do to help. The idea that came to me was that I could make peanut butter sandwiches.

I gathered together a group of ladies in our church to help me make sandwiches once a week. Then I spoke to Noleen, a missionary lady at our church who was feeding people in Phoenix, a predominantly Indian area on the border of Amaoti, and asked her how we could take the sandwiches into the township. She knew about the plight of the children in Amaoti and had been praying about going in to feed them. We joined forces and asked Pastor Derrick, who was working with Tich and the caddies, if he would go with Noleen to find and feed the children and minister to them in their own language.

Each week Noleen would come back and say that the number of children gathering for the sandwiches was increasing. I really wanted to go and see but I was too scared. As the weeks went by I knew I just had to overcome my fear so I asked Noleen to take me with her. Her reply was, "I am not going to take any white lady into a black township." I managed to convince her that it was important for me to take this step and she finally agreed. That was a huge turning point for me; I was no longer held back by my fears and very soon was in and out of the community all the time on my own.

A SHOCKING REALITY

I had an idea of what to expect but there's something very different about hearing that people are living in extreme poverty and seeing it with your own eyes. Going into Amaoti I was suddenly confronted with it up close, and although I had tried to prepare myself, the squalor was still a shock. The area was vast with hundreds upon hundreds of homes running all the way up the hillside and down into the valley. Most of the homes were broken down shacks, with many fallen into disrepair. The deeper you went, the worse the poverty was.

There was one area they called Tin City where shacks were crammed together with just tiny gaps between them. Buildings were seemingly thrown together with whatever was to hand: pieces of corrugated iron, mud, strips of old wood nailed haphazardly to one another. Roofs were cobbled together with bin bags or tarpaulin, weighted down with tyres and rocks to stop them blowing away in the wind. Homes that had small patches where they could grow vegetables were edged with broken fences. Those fortunate enough to have windows often had broken glass and old rags hanging as curtains.

There was filth like I have never seen before. Children, left to their own devices, ran around with bare feet and wearing dirty rags, their pot bellies advertising their starving bodies, their once black hair now paled showing their malnutrition. Teenage girls had swollen stomachs, their pregnancies a reminder that with little to do many started having sex at a young age. Many had been raped and abused and AIDS had spread quickly in the area.

The weight of hopelessness bore down heavily. What choices did people have living in this squalor? When their homes broke there was no way for them to pay for them to be repaired. When their clothes tore and their shoes fell apart, there was no money to replace them. Unemployment rates were sky high and many men would spend their time drinking themselves into a stupor to try and forget their woes.

It was no longer a group of faceless people dealing with these issues who I could easily choose not to think about; I was seeing individual faces, looking in their eyes, hearing their names and their stories, getting a glimpse into their lives, getting to know and love them. Sometimes we wait for God to give us compassion before we go to help people but often it's in the going that we find compassion comes. Once you've seen poverty like that you know you have to do more to stop it. Once you go you can't stop going.

Most of the people were suspicious of our motives. They would ask us why we were providing food; they felt sure we had to be getting something out of it. Some thought we were from the government and became very demanding, whilst others were welcoming and, despite the poverty, were extremely hospitable. There was an old lady who lived in one of the few brick and mortar homes who had a nice yard and invited us to feed the children there under her mango tree. Seeing the hunger on the children's faces as they lined up for their food, it quickly became clear that peanut butter sandwiches once a week were just a drop in the ocean in terms of meeting their need. We heard that the children were sometimes so famished they would eat cardboard that would swell up inside their stomachs and make them feel full. The thought was horrifying so we started making sandwiches every day and then decided to make soup too. We collected the peel of potatoes as the most nourishing part is just under the skin and used that as a base to try and get some goodness in them.

The first time we took soup we had no idea how many children would show up but we guessed about 50 as that's how many we'd been providing sandwiches for. We hadn't anticipated that word would get round so quickly that soup was on its way and soon there were over 100 kids hoping to eat. I looked at what we'd prepared and I looked at all the children, knowing instantly we didn't have enough but desperate that all those hungry stomachs would get filled. I said, "Lord, I don't want any child to go hungry; please don't let us run out." We served bowl after bowl of potato soup and I didn't dare look down into the container, I just concentrated on looking at the children and asking God to provide. When it came to the last little girl I dropped my gaze and sure enough there was just enough left for one last bowlful. What grace! Our faith increased that day and reminded us that God really does supply all our needs.

Most of the kids would come on their own, usually carrying younger brothers and sisters. Some would come with a mother or grandmother who were also starving and hoping we would be able to feed them, but we had to explain we didn't have enough for everyone and we were helping them by helping the children. To start with the children would line up waiting to be fed but the older ones would push the younger ones out of the way, knocking them over and hurting them in their haste to get to the food. We prayed and asked God what we should do to stop the chaos and he told us to read the story of the feeding of the five thousand. We thought we knew the story but as we re-read it we realised Jesus had got the crowd to sit down in small groups and then the disciples had served them. We learned a huge lesson, realising it broke the beggar mentality, stopped the chaos, and allowed everyone to eat without anyone getting hurt.

As the numbers grew, we moved to a small hall next door to the old lady's house which had been built for the express purpose of benefiting the community. It was an amazing gift to find such a facility in an area of poverty and soon the hall was filled with children coming to eat sandwiches and soup.

BACK TO SCHOOL

We began to question why so many of the children weren't in school and discovered their families couldn't afford the school fees or to buy the uniforms the children needed. We decided to start a back to school programme to get the children's education sponsored. I remember saying to the team we should take down the names of any orphans who weren't attending school, expecting there to be about 25, but word spread around Amaoti and soon there was a queue stretching down the street of people wanting to put their kids into school. One of the ladies from our church who was helping us said, "Joan, we can't sponsor more than 25," but I looked out at the sea of expectant little faces and said, "We can't stop. We have to keep going." By the time we had finished we had 125 on our list. She panicked but I was sure that God would provide. We went back to our local churches and shared the need with them. The response was overwhelming and soon every child was sponsored; God had provided.

The challenge I hadn't considered was whether schools would have capacity for so many children. We went from school to school in Amaoti and each said it was full; they couldn't take one child let alone 125. Finally, I ended up in the headmaster's office of the primary school in Brookdale, Phoenix, which neighboured Amaoti, and said I desperately needed his help. He instantly replied, "Send them to me." I tried to explain I had 125 children but he just laughed and promised he'd open new classrooms if need be.

Over the following few years we got 600 children on the back to school programme, finding places at 14 different schools. Some couldn't wait to get an education; others took a bit more persuading, as they weren't used to the discipline of school life. Many of the children's caregivers were used to having the children at home to do domestic chores so we had a battle on our hands there too, trying to educate them as to why it would benefit them in the long term. We started to employ youth workers and one of their responsibilities was to round the children up in the mornings and try and get them to school on time.

Outside of term time we began holiday clubs and were amazed that 1,500 children arrived on the first day. We also started ministry work with the women of Amaoti. A number would tell the children to steal from us, so desperate was their situation. Scripture teaches that we should not despise someone who steals because they are starving (Prov. 6:30), so we tried to work with them and help them see we could work together to change their circumstances.

Our church started a non-profit company (NPC) which we named Indlela, the Zulu word meaning "the way". An NPC is like a registered charity which we used to formalise our work in Amaoti and combine it with a babies' home and a counselling project the church was running. We started life skills training in different schools, and began a four-year HIV/AIDS prevention programme helping the children and teenagers to make better choices for their lives and teaching them godly principles. As the work in Amaoti grew we registered a separate charity which became Lungisani Indlela meaning "prepare the way".

ANNIE'S PLACE

To keep the little ones safe during the day we decided to start a crèche in the hall. Annie lived in the house next door to the old lady and she had four children and a newborn baby, all with different fathers, none of whom lived with her. As soon as we mentioned the crèche her face lit up and she gathered a group of women to help run it. In no time we had 100 children attending. Annie had helped us feed the children from the first day we arrived and now she became the headmistress of the crèche. She certainly had a gift. As we spent time with her, we told her about Jesus and she gave her life to him. The change was obvious to all who knew her.

One Saturday night the father of her youngest child came to her home. Annie's life had changed and she had turned her back on her old way of living. He stabbed her to death as she held her daughter in her arms. We were devastated. Annie was so special to us and to so many people, especially her five children, and it was such a tragic end to her life. We were so grateful that she knew Jesus and was in heaven, free from the difficulties and struggles she'd known on earth. Her funeral was a significant moment when the community came together and they saw us weeping at the loss of her precious life and realised we truly loved her and their community. We became one in our shared grief that day and became accepted members of the Amaoti community. We named the crèche Annie's Place and we will never forget her.

TICH'S FIRST VISIT TO AMAOTI

As I was spending more and more time in the community and with it becoming all-consuming, Tich thought he should come and see what his wife was doing. He came in to Amaoti on a sweltering hot and dusty day dressed in his insurance salesman smart suit. He met me at the crèche and the kids, at first unsure of this strange white man, were soon clambering at his legs and wanting to be picked up. One small boy he lifted up left a trail of snot all over the jacket of his suit, along with what had already been deposited on his trousers by the others. He handed the child back to me and said, "This isn't for me. I'll make the money and you can keep feeding the kids."

A few weeks later I had gone with a builder friend to look at a room we wanted to rent for storage space. We found ourselves walking into the middle of a taxi strike. Tensions were running high and the situation seemed volatile. We hesitated but decided to proceed as I had a real sense of peace. Soon afterwards a car with two men stopped alongside us and asked us what we were doing there, one was an Australian man and the other an African. It was quite surreal. I

asked them the same question and Joe, the African man, said he was
showing his friend around Amaoti. They wanted to bring others and
asked if they could film what we were doing in the township. We
arranged to meet them there on the Saturday morning. I asked Tich
to go with me as I had never been into Amaoti on a Saturday and felt
unsure about our safety.

That Saturday we met Mike Pilavachi, from Soul Survivor in
the UK, and Hugh Evans, who began the Oaktree Foundation in
Australia. I wasn't sure what to make of Mike, who looked like a
Greek but spoke like an Englishman. We had no idea that it would
be the start of a lifelong journey of friendship and caring together for
poor and broken children in Durban.

It was the first time Mike had set foot in a township and he
was speechless (something that we've since discovered is a rare occur-
rence!). We walked into the bowels of Amaoti, travelling the small
uneven pathways between the huts as there were no roads between
them. Mike and Hugh filmed with their team as they walked and
a growing number of children began to follow. Mike became like
the Pied Piper, gathering a large crowd, and we sang as we walked.
Suddenly two young girls ran out of a shebeen.[1] One was cradling
her arm in her skirt as blood poured out. It was a surreal moment of
thinking, *Did I really just see that?*

Tich entered the bar and Mike and Hugh followed, thinking it
must be OK if Tich was going in, not realising this was only Tich's
second time in the township and he'd never been in one of these bars
before. It was 10 a.m. and some of the guys in there were already

---

1   An illegal bar.

drunk, whilst others were hanging around playing pool. Tich began to tell them about Jesus. Some became angry, others stopped and listened. But the person who God spoke to the clearest that day was Tich himself. When he agreed to come with me to Amaoti that day, two miracles happened. All he knew was that he was sacrificing a game of golf—which was the first miracle; he had no idea God was about to break his heart for the destitute and the lost and change his life forever.

VALENTINO'S STORY

Valentino was born one hot September day in Amaoti. When she was five years old her mother, who had just qualified as a journalist, was killed in a car accident whilst on her way to start a job near Johannesburg. The last time she saw her father was at the funeral of her mother. Living with her grandmother she managed to cling on to the hope that her circumstances might change, and when we met her in 2006 she was desperate to be a part of our back to school programme. We got her a place at Brookdale High School in Phoenix and found a sponsor to pay for her text books, stationery, uniform and school fees. She worked hard, studying by candlelight late into the night as she held on to her dream to follow in her mother's footsteps. In all the years she lived in Amaoti she never went out of the mud shack they called home after dark for fear of being raped.

One of the proudest moments of our lives was hearing that Valentino had gained six distinctions in her matric exams.[2] We met with Professor Jansen, the vice chancellor of the University of the Free State, told him her story, and showed him her results. He said, "Send her to me," and arranged for a full bursary for her to study journalism there. Valentino completed her four-year degree in three years. The professor said in all the years he had been in education he had never come across a student who had so positively influenced a campus and staff the way she did.

Valentino defied all the odds. She went against the grain and proved that when given an opportunity, anyone can turn their life around. Valentino continues to make a difference in the lives of others as she embarks on the new season of her life as a journalist. She has the potential to be a world changer. We realised there must be so many more Valentinos out there in the townships waiting for an opportunity to shine. All they need is a helping hand.

When grace showed up for Valentino in her mud shack with no electricity, she embraced it.

One day, we have no doubt, you will be reading her book.

---

2   The exams taken in the final year of school.

PART III

Released

Chapter 7

A CHANGE OF HEART

*Trust in the L*ORD *and do good; dwell in the land and enjoy safe pasture.*

Psalm 37:3

Tich

Although Joan had been working in Amaoti for about six months and it was taking up more and more of her time, it wasn't something I had imagined I would ever get involved in. I'd continued my ministry with the caddies and between that, work, church, golf and family life, I felt I was "doing my bit". When I did venture into the township with Joan I noticed straight away that the community was suspicious of white people and many of the smaller children were terrified of men because they'd suffered so much abuse. They would run away screaming while the older ones would hang around, wondering who you were and why you were there. As Joan has said, it didn't take long till some had warmed to me, but getting covered in snot was not my idea of a good time, and it was only when I went back to Amaoti for the second time that God changed my heart. I knew I had to come back to the community to share the love of Jesus with them.

When I was confronted with the drunken men in the shebeen, I was initially angry. Many had no work, and the area was so poor that we were feeding their children, and yet they still found money for alcohol and drugs. However, as someone who suffered under addictions I knew they were in a desperate place. I asked them their stories and told them about Jesus and as I left I felt God say to me, "They are as vulnerable to the gospel as they are to the things of the world, but no one is offering them the gospel."

For the first time I wept over the brokenness and poverty of the lives in the Amaoti community. I looked at the faces of the women and children who lived there and my heart broke to think that they couldn't leave their homes at night for fear of being raped and abused. I heard about tiny babies who had been violated because some men believed that sex with a virgin would cure them of AIDS. Lives that were so precious to God were being destroyed and I could no longer live in my comfortable home on the beach and pretend it wasn't happening. I had heard about the poverty through Joan of course but when I saw it for myself God broke my heart and I knew there was no turning back.

MEN'S GROUPS

My friend Blake and I began to go into Amaoti every Friday afternoon and meet with a group of men under the mango tree where Joan had first started feeding the children. As we chatted to them we began to see how hopeless they felt. Many had long since stopped looking for work; what was the point when there was no work to be found? We asked them how they managed to survive and were amazed at their answer. They told us that those who were employed would share their food with those in need. We had gone there to minister to these men but soon found that they were ministering to us as well. Here were biblical principles being lived out in the most difficult situations. We were convicted that day that we really didn't know much about sharing God's way.

Most in the community were unemployed and many of these men were members of gangs who were involved in hideous crimes, including the rape and abuse of women and children. They were desperate enough to steal from their own and many were addicted to alcohol and drugs. A small group gathered to meet with us initially, whilst others would come without participating, just to try to work out what we were doing. We got to know them, would bring food to eat together, and spent time chatting about their lives before sharing from the Bible and offering to pray for them. When we told them about Jesus some were sceptical, wondering if this Jesus was going to turn up with a bread van, ready to feed their families. Others accepted Jesus wholeheartedly. One was a gangster called Soldier who had only known a life of crime. He was feared in the community, but when he gave his life to Jesus everyone could see the turnaround. He began evangelising to anyone and everyone and stood up for righteousness. The transformation was so profound that we soon asked him to join our team as a youth worker in the crèches we were supporting, and he even started to assist Pastor Derrick at the church.

TEETHING TROUBLES

Rather than just giving handouts I wanted to use my experience to help some of the men and women start their own businesses so they could get a steady income and also provide jobs for others. I looked for entrepreneurs that I could come alongside, and started with a block plant[1] business run as a cooperative with six shareholders consisting of four men and two women. I invested capital into the business and initially it prospered as all six enthusiastically played their part.

Instead of them earning an income from the profits, I paid them salaries which turned out to be a big mistake! Very soon we noticed the men would sit and watch while the women worked like slaves. When I mentioned it was time for them to pay me back for the capital investment they didn't agree and took me to their lawyer. The lawyer took one look at the situation, laughed, and confirmed to them they did indeed have to start paying me back. Over the next few years they were able to repay the loan but it was another tough lesson learnt along the journey. I was desperate to do the right thing but was new and naive in my approach.

We hadn't expected there to be so much suspicion about our motives either, and we began to realise that mistrust is a huge hurdle to overcome. Though apartheid had long since ended it had of course sown huge divisions between the races and many feared that white people would only want to use and abuse them as this is all they had known in the past.

---

1   A simple, manual method for producing bricks for building.

GLIMMERS OF HOPE

One day I met a true entrepreneur by the name of Anna. She was running a small restaurant out of a container on the main road of Amaoti,
providing traditional African meals to passers-by. She approached me
to help her to grow her business and we bought her another container
so she could increase the number of tables. Soon after Anna called to
say her husband, Derek, was desperately ill and appeared to be suffering
from the AIDS virus. He had become painfully thin, his eyes hollow,
and he had no energy so was unable to work. Pastor Derrick and I went
to pray for him and a month later when we went to see how he was
doing, he was back at work and once more full of energy. To this day
he has never looked back. This was the start of their journey with Jesus.

Anna's business continued to grow as we walked alongside them,
but a few years later when I stopped by, Anna's husband told me she
was now desperately sick and he took us to their house. We were
shocked to see Anna in bed, her body wasting away in the same manner as Derek's had been. She was dying and it broke my heart. I got
down on my knees beside her bed and begged God to heal her from
this dreadful disease. A month later I went back to see if there was any
change in her condition and Derek took me to the local hair salon.
There was a healthy and happy Anna, smiling from ear to ear whilst
having her hair done!

A PLACE TO WORSHIP

As we continued with feeding thousands of children in the 27
crèches we were supporting, working with the 600 children

on the back to school programme, and running men's groups and a soccer league we had started, we began to feel like there should be a gathering in Amaoti on a Sunday. We wanted to get everyone together to celebrate God's goodness, so we prayed for someone to lead the church. I usually sleep like a baby but one morning I woke up at 2 a.m. and felt God say that we should stop praying for someone to plant the church as he wanted us to do it.

I argued that I didn't speak the language (something I now wish I had learned to honour the community), and we had never been actively involved in leadership of a church let alone thought about planting one. But I knew it was no use; God had spoken and we just had to get on and do it. We asked some church leaders, "What is a church supposed to do?" They said that most churches don't do what God wants them to do anyway so, "Just go and do what God has called you to do!"

We planted the church in the same place we had the first crèche, and on that initial Sunday we had over 100 people. I thought, *Wow, I'm going to build such a big church!* Three weeks later God told me that we needed to preach and teach against the animal sacrifice and ancestral worship that was so prevalent in the area. We knew it wouldn't be right for us to share that message so we asked a young black leader to preach it as it would be easier to hear it from him. It didn't go down well. The following Sunday there were just 10 people left in the congregation. For almost a year we had those same 10 people and we questioned what we were doing but God simply told us to persevere and he would build his church.

ANCESTRAL WORSHIP

Joan

Ancestral worship ran deep in the community and I was about to see up close the hold it had on people. A lady called Angela approached me for help with her crèche and the orphans she was looking after in Amaoti. She told me she had been a sangoma but said her "powers" had mysteriously left her, meaning she was unable to work and earn money. We became friends and I told her we should pray and ask Jesus to help us raise the funds she needed.

She invited me for tea at her home which consisted of one room with a curtain in the middle dividing the living and kitchen area from the bedroom. The toilet was a pit outside. Angela had three children of her own and had taken in three orphans, two of whom were disabled. She also said she took in others who were dying of AIDS when their families didn't want to care for them anymore; there was still a huge stigma attached to the AIDS virus.

When she showed me behind the curtain where her bedroom area was, my heart sank. I saw a piece of skin from a sacrificed animal hanging over her bed. I asked her about it, knowing full well that she was relying on this to ward off evil spirits. She replied, "This is my culture." I cried out to God in my heart, "Help me, Father, what can I, a white woman, say to her that will set her free from this bondage?"

What came out of my mouth I knew was God's wisdom and not my own. "Angela," I said, "my culture was apartheid. My ancestors taught me that this was right, that we were superior to people of colour, but there came a time when we had to say 'no more' to our ancestors and have the courage to change. Our God is a jealous God; he is waiting outside your house. He cannot come into your home and into your life while you are trusting your ancestors and the skins of animals to protect you and provide for you. We all have to make choices every day. In every culture there is good and bad stuff. God wants us to discard the bad and embrace and celebrate the good." She immediately took the skin down and threw it outside and on the way home I prayed that she would make the right choice knowing she could so easily put the skin back again once I had left.

Two weeks later she told me that her eldest son had said to her, "Mama, all these years we have been trusting in our ancestors to help us and we have had nothing from them, maybe we should try Jesus." The next week we received unexpected funds from the UK from people we'd never met. We were able to add two bedrooms onto Angela's house, build a proper toilet, and improve her crèche facilities where she was looking after over 100 children daily. As Angela put all her trust in Jesus, he showed up and answered her prayers.

NEW ROOTS

Tich

The highs and lows of all of this took their toll. Many times we wondered if we were really managing to achieve anything at all. I remember one morning I had an argument with one of the community leaders and I drove away saying, "Lord, I don't have to put up with this. We're trying to help and people don't appreciate it. I'm not going to do it anymore." God spoke to me very clearly saying, "I was mocked, scorned and nailed to the cross; never speak to me about offence again. Just get over it."

We also realised we needed much deeper roots in God to be able to cope with all that was going on. We were introduced to an amazing woman called Ann who had been in full-time ministry for more than 20 years, ministering to and training young people in the communities. We asked her to come and do some training with our team in Amaoti and instantly connected with her. She became like a mentor to us and we met every week as she helped us journey through what God was calling us to do. We weren't convinced we had it in us but she kept reminding us that if God had called us, he would equip us. She was also clear that God was calling us to do this together and that we had to grow in working side by side so that our marriage was strong enough to sustain our ministry.

She would speak very directly to us and, though it was sometimes hard, it was exactly what we needed. She was unafraid to challenge us, especially when it came to how much time we were spending with God, and she helped us lay some healthy foundations to our relationship with Jesus. I began to regularly spend time with my Father, filling journals as I wrote both my prayers and what I felt God was saying in response, sometimes praying and reading my Bible for hours at a time. It was a complete turnaround for the man who became a Christian and then never set foot in a church for four years.

GATES OF BETRAYAL

Joan

When we walk closely in the footsteps of Jesus we too have to go through gates of betrayal. For Jesus this led to death, but for us God can use it for our good to bring us into new life. It can be like giving birth: painful but ultimately fruitful. A number of times people have come to me saying they've had dreams that I'm pregnant. At my age, I'm thankful this has been God speaking about spiritual changes that are coming and not about physical babies! Most of us want the new things but don't want to go through the birthing pains to get there and when things get tough we can be tempted to quit before we see the breakthrough. For us in Amaoti, though the projects were continuing to multiply, we were entering into a time of pain.

A group of unemployed young adults from the community came to volunteer with us after completing three months of intensive, life-changing training and discipleship with the World Changers Academy (WCA), run by an American missionary and his Zulu wife. Over the next few years we journeyed with them, teaching them and guiding them and they became our hands and feet with the children. As funding came in, we were able to pay them salaries and we grew to love them as our own; they even called us Mom and Dad. One of the young guys, Francis, came to work in our garden. A missionary couple staying with us at the time said God was showing them that Francis was a danger to us but we didn't think it could ever be true. He was like our son and we were sure he'd never do anything to hurt us. The next day another friend called to say she had dreamt about me and felt I was in danger and needed to be careful. When the third person told me the same thing I realised I needed to be alert.

The following Friday morning I was about to head off to Amaoti as usual. I got into the car, turned the ignition and then stopped. Without really thinking about what I was doing I switched off the engine, got out of my car, went back inside and told Tich I had decided not to go that day. A week later the pastor of a local church where some of the team went, asked to meet with us and when we arrived we could see the anger written all over his face. "How dare you?" he said, clearly furious. We were shocked and asked him what we had done to cause such offence. "You've taken money that was given for the young people of Amaoti and you've used it for yourselves!"

It was like being hit by a train. We were stunned and horrified that anyone could think we would do something so underhand and despicable. I sobbed and sobbed that these young people who were like sons and daughters to us would even believe such a thing. We realised there was still so much mistrust; everyone was always looking for our ulterior motives, not believing we would help without trying to gain from it ourselves. We have no idea how the rumour started but perhaps having seen our home and two cars, Francis had told his friends and the suspicion had grown from there. We later found out that the day I had changed my mind at the last minute about going in to the community there were two guys who'd been lying in wait for "the white woman with all the money" to arrive.

When people asked me why I wasn't afraid to go into such a dangerous community I had always said that I have the faith to believe that when God sees we are in danger, he will pull us out. I knew this was one of those moments when, for no logical reason, I changed my mind about going into Amaoti and it had been God's grace keeping me safe.

Once the pastor realised that the rumours had no basis he started setting people straight but we knew deep inside that God was removing us from Amaoti and we didn't think we could ever go back into the community again. We handed the church we had planted, and the projects, over to Pastor Derrick and his wife, Maureen.

Three months later God spoke to us through Psalm 37, telling us not to fret about those who were intent on doing wrong and to "trust in the LORD and do good; dwell in the land and enjoy safe pasture" (v. 3). To our surprise we felt he was telling us we were to go back into Amaoti. Slowly we started going back and re-establishing relationships, but all the young team we had been working with had disappeared. Over time some of them started to come back one by one in repentance, wanting to work with us again. Others, including Francis, we never saw again. It was like they vanished as it says in Psalm 37, "Soon you will see them no more" (v. 10).

This gate of betrayal was the most painful of all because of our growing love for them, but true to his word, God began to work all things together for good according to his plan and purpose. What the enemy had intended for harm, God had used for good. The situation actually deepened the trust people had in us and our relationships grew even stronger than before. It was a lesson for us that if God sends you somewhere, there's no safer place for you to be.

Chapter 8

PITCH A TENT, PREACH THE GOSPEL

Go into all the world and preach the gospel to all creation.

Mark 16:15

Tich

One day I was praying over the community from the local sports field, looking out over the mud shacks, and heard God say that shacks would come down, houses would go up and thousands would come to know him. He said, "Pitch a tent and preach the gospel for 28 days to bring reconciliation between me and my people and between the races." I immediately knew he wanted the tent to be pitched in the buffer zone between Amaoti and Phoenix that had been created during the apartheid era to separate the different races.

Everyone thought I had lost my mind. Sure, people sometimes ran evangelistic events for a weekend or maybe even a week at a time but 28 days? We didn't even know how to go about planning it. All I knew was that God was saying it had to be in October although that also didn't make any sense as that's the start of our rainy season. We sat down with a blank page and asked God to fill it. Each night we would need someone to preach, someone to lead worship and 100 volunteers to make things run smoothly; where were they all going to come from?

Three years earlier, in 2004, God had given me a vision to hold a business breakfast at the International Convention Centre to lift the name of Jesus in the market place. I had approached many churches in and around the Durban area and over 80 supported the breakfast so we approached the same churches again to come on board with the crusade. Leaders from around the country began to offer the support we needed, offering to cover days and sometimes weeks at a time, and the blank pages began to fill up.

God had said thousands would come to know him so we knew we had to get a big tent! We bought a 5,000-seater Big Top and erected it in the buffer zone. We also planted a huge cross made of solid steel in the ground outside the tent. It was so heavy that it took 30 men to carry it. (We placed it in concrete to keep it secure and after the event no one could get it out so it's still standing there today!) We wanted to light up the cross so it could be seen from miles around. Without thinking it through I attached strip lights around the outline of the cross, then ran an electrical connection from Pastor Derrick's home, some 100 metres away. Unsurprisingly, given the fact that the cross was huge and I'd plugged it in to a household socket, some months after the crusade the light fixtures burst into flames (and also blew out the power in Derrick's house)! Many people from Amaoti called us that night to tell us the cross was burning up on the hillside. The blackened cross still remains today as a reminder to all the people about the month when grace showed up in Amaoti.

A HEAVENLY FLOOD

The first night of the crusade the heavens opened and the rain came down, flooding the tent until there were inches of water on the floor, but amazingly no one seemed to notice. It was like God was cleansing the place and we all praised and worshipped with no regard for the weather. I was the MC and that evening we knew it was important to demonstrate unity between the races so we had an African, an Indian and Joan as a white South African pray together on the stage. They each shared about how they felt and then prayed over the gathered group but when Joan's turn came she just wept. Full of the Holy Spirit she got down on her knees and cried and cried, repenting publicly for all that white South Africans had done to oppress the other races and mourning the wickedness of the apartheid system. It was an incredible moment, reminiscent of Isaiah repenting on behalf of Israel. What a way to start the crusade!

Each night the community came in their thousands, many young children came completely unsupervised, and thousands upon thousands came to know Jesus. It was the craziest thing I had ever been involved in and it was the best month of my life. Gathering the community in such large numbers inevitably meant there was some trouble between the gangs, and one night some of the music equipment was stolen, but nothing could dampen our joy that so many were being saved. God built his church as he said he would with some of those who came to know him during that month.

God had provided for us in amazing ways and we had some of the best musicians and preachers in the country, as well as an abundance of volunteers from 70 different churches. On that first night when the rain was so heavy that all the cars got stuck in the mud on the school sports field, the Sharks rugby team, who were among the volunteers, stayed until midnight helping to get them free, literally picking them up and pushing them forward. Our eyes were opened to the greatness of God in a new way; we could never have orchestrated such an event ourselves and we were more determined than ever to follow and obey God whatever he called us to do.

Joan

In the run up to the crusade, we had tried to get permission to erect our Big Top in the buffer zone. This wasn't easy and we were advised that it's sometimes better to ask for forgiveness than permission. So we went ahead, digging into the hill with bulldozers and changing the shape of the hill on government-owned land! After the crusade had ended, Tich was summoned to meet the councillor of Amaoti to discuss what we had done.

As he was unable to attend he sent me in his place and when I walked into her office her entire council was there too. The atmosphere was immediately tense and I knew I was in big trouble. I could feel the hatred and anger as they started to shout and ask me who we thought we were that we would just move onto government property and do as we pleased with it. They were rightly furious that we had gone ahead without permission and as such had shown them so little respect. As they continued to scold me I had two warring emotions. The loudest thought was, *Just get up and walk out. You don't have to sit here and listen to this. Get out of Amaoti; they aren't grateful for anything you are doing to help the people. Just go.* The other, quieter, voice was whispering, *Just say you're sorry.*

When they were finally finished and they asked me what I had to say, I knew I had to make a choice as to which voice I was going to listen to. I felt a surge of compassion and love, as well as tremendous repentance and pain—just as I had done on the first night of the crusade—for what we as white people had done. As I started to say sorry, the floodgates welled up from deep within my inner being and I began to sob uncontrollably. I asked them to forgive us for our arrogance and all the hurt and pain we had caused every black person over the years. I could barely get the words out in between my tears.

When I finally calmed down and looked at them, their eyes were like saucers, and the lady next to me was patting my back, trying to console me and tell me it was OK. The Holy Spirit had changed the atmosphere and it was a healing moment for all of us. The love of Christ had shown up in that tiny, swelteringly hot office, and it had pushed back the darkness that had threatened to envelop us.

The reconciliation was so strong that a few weeks later they invited me to sit at the head table on the stage during a community function and told the gathered crowd that I had earned the right to be there. It was surreal, finding myself sitting at a table that displayed the flag of the African National Congress (ANC). I briefly considered what my ancestors would have thought if they could have seen me associated with a party they had believed to be terrorists. I think I became an honorary member of the ANC that day. It was a very humbling moment and I felt God was building a bridge much stronger than any we could have built with human effort.

The government is now using the land that we had levelled, and has built a transitional camp whilst they build new houses for the community. This fulfils the vision God gave Tich when he said, "Shacks will come down, houses will go up and thousands will come to know me." God truly does work in mysterious ways and once again he'd taken our arrogance in using government land without permission and used it for good.

(L-R) Tich with dad, Gerald, and brother, Guy, 1973

Celebrating their mother's 70th birthday (L-R) Guy, Peggy, Sue (sister), and Tich

Tich with (L-R) brother Guy and cousins Shorts and Patrick on golf tour in Scotland, 2009

The Waring family, Bunty and Billie with their three daughters, Felicity, Amanda and Joan (in front)

Joan's parents, Billie and Bunty Waring, at their 50th wedding anniversary

Celebrating with Joan (2nd left) at her 40th are sisters Amanda and Felicity, with their mum

Joan (front 2nd left) winning the inter-schools' hockey tournament, 1966—highlight of her school career

Some of Tich's sporting career highlights. The "new caps" are for rugby

Tich sharing a joke with Clive Rice (former South Africa captain) during a cup final, 1978

Tich (back left) representing South Africa, 1973

Tich (left) and his Natal teammates enjoying another Currie Cup victory, 1976

Scoring the winning runs for Natal in victory over a "rest of South Africa" team, 1976

Tich (front left), age 7, seated alongside brother Guy, in the under-10 cricket team

Tich the all-rounder in action

Joan in Natal golf champi-onship final, 1990

Love ruled out Bok honours

The Argus Bureau: London, Wednesday.

SOUTH AFRICAN golf girl Joan Waring will soon be lining up on the British professional circuit — as a caddie.

Joan, 22-year-old niece of the Minister of Sport (Mr Frank Waring) plays in next week's British Women's Championship at Hunstanton, Norfolk.

Then she will put her clubs away and take charge of the bag belonging to Springbok pro Vince Baker, to whom she became engaged in February.

And one thing is certain. Joan, a petite blonde, will be no novelty among the South African players.

Already Joan Batocchi is caddying for husband Hugh, Marie Britz for husband Tienie, Margaret Purvis for husband-to-be Terry Westbrook, and Dannielle de Marsche for Gary Baleson.

Soon Helen Bland will fly in to swell the 'army' still further by caddying for her husband.

Joan Waring gave up the chance of Springbok honours in the world team champion-ships in Buenos Aires in October to be with her 26-year-old fiance, whom she met during the 1971 Western Province Open. She arrived in Britain six weeks ago and is working as a

ARGIE

'I hope Joan won't find caddying a W(e)aring experience!'

radiologist at London's new Hampstead Hospital.

'After the British Women's she'll join me for the Sun-beam event and the Open in Scotland, then we're going to the Continent for the French, Swiss, German and Dutch Opens,' explained Vince.

Joan the caddie, 1972

Joan at 17 reaching the semi-finals of her first Western Province championship, 1967

Tich and Joan at daughter Katie's wedding, 2004

Tich and Joan on their wedding day, 14th June 1991

Celebrating at the reception, one year later

Bringing two families together: Tich and Joan with children Greg, Julie, Grant, and Katie

Grant and his wife, Kate, with baby Billi Baker, 2016

Julie and husband, Andrew, with Sebastian and Luca

Greg and Kirst with little Molly, Anna, and Tommy

Katie and husband, Curtis, with Ben and Jack

The gathering of the "clan" at the beach house to celebrate Grant and Kate's wedding, April 2015

AMAOTI

Humble mud shack and dirt road typifies life in Amaoti

Annie's crèche: children carrying chairs for story time under the tree

Breaking down Annie's shack to build a home for her five children after she was killed

Tich and Joan with Pastor Derrick, praying for healing at the church they started in Amaoti, 2005

Tich praying with his regular group of men under the mango tree

Thousands came to know Jesus during the 28 nights of the crusade

Prayer at the opening of the crusade, representing the different races of South Africa

A 5,000-seater tent for the Amaoti crusade

The cross planted on the hill at the crusade, which still remains today, towering over Amaoti

THE BUILDING OF THE VILLAGE BEGINS...

Tich and friend Blake surveying the land before the building of the village begins, 2009

Tich, Derrick and builders praying over the foundations of the first homes

KZN Premier Dr. Zweli Mkhize visits LIV village, 2010

Converting the broken-down chicken sheds into the school classrooms and hall, 2010

(L-R) Mama Dudu and Mlondi, saying goodbye to her mother before moving to LIV as a foster mother, 2011

The building of the multi-purpose church hall / indoor sports centre and admin block, 2013

THE LIV BANQUET 2010 — FEEDING THE 4,000

Tich escorting Premier Dr. Mkhize and Mayor Obed Mlaba, surrounded by bodyguards

Preparing for the banquet at the ICC. This is just half of the 250-metre-long hall!

MC Shaun Pollock (former SA cricket captain) assisted by John Smit (former SA rugby captain)

Everyone was fed from 17 kitchens and 44 buffet stations, with plenty left over

LIFE IN THE VILLAGE – BECOMING FAMILY

LIV children praying for one another, the supernatural becoming natural for them

Children join staff for devotions

Food distribution in the early days

Typical children's bedroom

Each day starts with early morning prayers in the clusters

The opening of LIV School, August 2011: five pupils and two volunteer teachers, Monica (L) from Norway and Bronwyn from Canada

LIV family and friends celebrate together at the opening of the new church hall, June 2015

Baba Smith enjoying lunch with some of the girls at LIV School

Tich and Joan love being Baba and Gogo to the LIV children

Enjoying life at LIV

Harvesting the first "fruits" from the vegetable garden

Gogo Smith chilling out in the farmhouse with some of the LIV family

LIV CELEBRATIONS

"Women of Worth" lavish tea party for 550 ladies with Carita interviewing Joan, Kimberley Johnson, Rachel Lungu, and Ann Moodley, June 2015

Joan celebrating Women's Day in traditional dress with "daughters" (L-R) Grace, Priscilla, Dudu and Kitty, who are LIV mamas

LIV banquet #2: 700 guests come to the village to celebrate the vision becoming a reality, June 2015

LIV School choir

Mothers and children giving thanks to Jesus at the village banquet

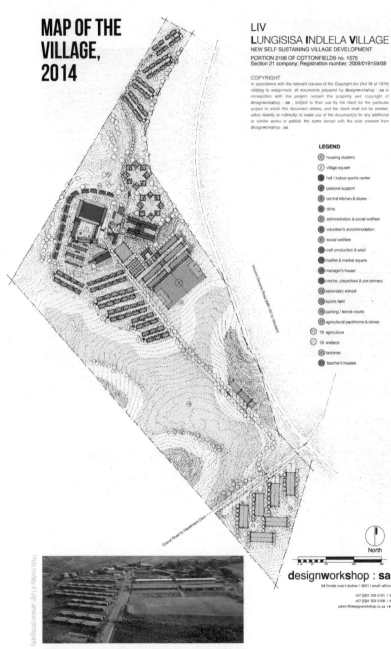

MAP OF THE
VILLAGE,
2014

LIV
LUNGISISA **I**NDLELA **V**ILLAGE
NEW SELF SUSTAINING VILLAGE DEVELOPMENT
PORTION 2198 OF COTTONFIELDS no. 1575
Section 21 company; Registration number: 2009/019159/08

LEGEND

1. housing clusters
2. village square
3. hall / indoor sports center
4. pastoral support
5. central kitchen & stores
6. clinic
7. administration & social welfare
8. volunteer's accommodation
9. social welfare
10. craft production & retail
11. market & market square
12. manager's house
13. creche, playschool & pre-primary
14. secondary school
15. sports field
16. parking / tennis courts
17. agricultural packhome & stores
18. agriculture
19. wetland
20. factories
21. teacher's houses

North

designworkshop : sa

94 florida road I durban I 4001 I south africa

+27 (0)31 303 5191 I t
+27 (0)31 303 5198 I f
admin@designworkshop.co.za I e

LIV in 2015, which has capacity for 1,000 children

LIV AND FRIENDS — TOGETHER WE CAN...

Tich and Joan present Mike Pilavachi at Soul Survivor Watford with a vuvuzela (traditional instrument blown by supporters at soccer games in South Africa)

Mike interviewing Tich and Joan on stage during the Soul Survivor festival, 2015

Tich and Mike (in an African shirt made in the LIV factory) at the Soul Survivor festival, 2012

LIV Sports Ambassadors wearing their LIV wristbands with pride

Chapter 9

THE TIME IS NOW

For the vision is yet for an appointed time, but at the
end it shall speak, and not lie: though it tarry, wait for
it; because it will surely come, it will not tarry.

Habakkuk 2:3 (KJV)

Tich

Joan and I had been planning our retirement for some time. We had pictured ourselves living out our twilight season spending half the year at Fancourt Golf Estate in George, a town nestled beneath the Outeniqua Mountains along the Cape Garden Route, and the cooler winter months in Durban at our beach house. We thought we had it all worked out.

We were in our mid-50s, and had been building the house at Fancourt for over a year, going back and forth for site meetings and to pick out the finishes we wanted. When the house was finally completed we enjoyed our first few holidays in our new home.

Our families came to visit, we played golf every day, and relaxed on our veranda facing the beautiful mountains and overlooking one of the four golf courses. It was self-indulgence to the limit. After the first year of travelling between the two houses, we found ourselves sitting on our veranda admiring the view but feeling exceedingly bored. We were both hit with the same feeling: what are we doing here when we should be in Amaoti? We packed our bags, rented the house out for a year and then sold it; we had completely lost the desire to go back.

We had planned our future without consulting our heavenly Father; perhaps because we weren't sure we would like his plans as much as our own! We finally came to our senses and realised that there is no such thing as retirement in the Bible. Instead God's Word says we will "still bear fruit in old age" (Ps. 92:14) and, knowing we were called to help the destitute and broken, the widow and the orphan, we repented of our foolishness and returned to Durban and Amaoti. All the time God was graciously watching, and probably laughing at us, these two cracked pots of his making crazy choices. He knew we needed to get these worldly desires out of our system before he led us into the next season he had planned for us.

PASSING THE BATON

When I had asked the well-known evangelist Angus Buchan to come and preach at the crusade, he had said he would come on one condition: that I read his latest book. It was called *Passing the Baton* and was about when he handed his farm over to his sons. I was keen to read it as Angus's faith has always inspired me, but I had no idea that God was about to speak so profoundly to me through it. As I read it I felt God say that I should give our son, Greg, the business to run and go into the community full-time. Although I enjoyed the work I was doing in Amaoti I never visualised myself going in every day, but the message was so clear that I knew I had to obey. The business had been going well but I could see that it had gone from needing someone with strong sales experience like me, to someone with excellent administration skills like Greg. He'd been working with me for the previous seven years so it was a natural handover as he knew the company inside and out.

It was a difficult time for me having been in the insurance industry for the previous 25 years and suddenly finding myself with no office to go to, though I watched with pride as Greg grew the business into something very special. I could see that God knew the end from the beginning and that when we are obedient to his call, he will work things out far better than we ever could.

Our work in Amaoti was increasing daily but a year later God spoke to me very clearly and said I was to clear my desk and spend time with him. I ignored it. I felt like I'd given up everything and was already in the community full-time; surely God wasn't asking more of me? Soon after that, while I was on the bike at the gym, God said, "Do you love me enough to stop?" "Stop what, Lord?" I asked. "Stop everything," came the reply. I went back home to tell Joan and she said, "Now you're hearing from the devil! There's so much to do. We're employing 20 young people, we're supporting so many crèches looking after little ones, we're feeding over 2,000 children every day; we've even planted a church. How can we give it up?" I had no answer, but on 9th

January 2009 God said, "Now is the time for the village." We passed the baton to the young people we'd been raising up in Amaoti and went away for five weeks to rest and spend time with Jesus.

The first thing we felt God was asking us to do was to work on our marriage. "Oh no, Lord, we're doing just fine," we tried to tell him. "We want to focus on what you want us to do for you." But the nagging feeling continued and so grudgingly we began to look at all the little things that had been eating away at our marriage. We realised God was still refining us and helping us communicate better with each other. We had got into bad habits of running around with our busy lives and when we hit bumps in the road we just tried to ignore them and carry on. With so much time off we didn't have any excuses and had to start looking at why we were always arguing, getting irritated with each other, and speaking harshly to each other. We so easily see the flaws in others yet have so many blind spots when it comes to our own faults. We remembered what Peter Pollock's wife, Inez, said to us when we first got married, "Give 100 per cent and expect nothing in return and you will always be content." That's God's recipe for a happy marriage, but his ways are diametrically opposed to the world's; our sinful nature constantly tells us we should be receiving what we want, not giving everything we can. I can't say either of us enjoyed having to face up to what was going on but we knew God was strengthening our marriage for what lay ahead.

FINDING THE LAND

It had been 12 years since God had first spoken about the village and the picture had been in the back of our minds all that time. We had often wondered if the township was what God had meant, but the image I'd seen was so clear that we knew it didn't quite fit. Many of us experience what can feel like lengthy delays between God giving us a vision and it coming to fruition but he is always working in the background, even when it can seem like nothing is happening. When God first spoke to us we immediately tried to make things happen in our own strength and we got nowhere. In the intervening years God had been dealing with us, teaching us and moulding us through all that we experienced in Amaoti until we knew that the only way to get anything done was to be completely dependent on him and him alone. We could also see some of our practical circumstances had changed dramatically over the preceding 12 years. First of all, our finances were in a completely different place. I had paid off all of my debts and, thanks to the success of the business, we were able to look at buying the land ourselves instead of trying to get the government to give it. The other interesting change was that there was a new Premier of KwaZulu-Natal who had a real heart for the orphan.[1]

We didn't have a clue where to start but as I spent time with God, he began to speak clearly, giving me names of people to contact, some of whom I had never even met. One gentleman was Murray Armstrong, who we knew by name as he went to our church. We approached Murray and told him that God said he would be able to help us find the land for the village. Murray took this calling very seriously and unbeknown to us, his family had been farmers in the area for six generations. He knew every inch of the terrain, and spent

---

1   Each province (state) in South Africa has a Premier who governs the province with a cabinet.

the next six months taking us all over the area looking at potential farms. Many times Joan would ask me from the back of the car, "Do you feel anything?" as we looked at a piece of land but I felt nothing. I had the picture so clearly in my head as to what the land would look like and we hadn't found it yet. The other thing God had told me was to build the church first, but wherever we looked there were no people to preach to, only hectares of sugar cane!

During that time, we had been invited to share our vision at Soul Survivor in the UK. Whilst we'd met Mike Pilavachi, who heads up Soul Survivor, a number of times by this point, it had always been here in South Africa so we'd never seen the events he runs in action. It was quite something to arrive in the south west of England and find that a huge agricultural showground had been turned into the venue for an event for 10,000 young people! Every morning and evening everyone gathered together in a huge tent for times of worship and ministry in the power of the Holy Spirit and we were blown away. It was incredible to be in a place where God was able to move so freely and people worshipped so passionately. You hear about the church dying out in places like the UK and then you see thousands of young people passionately praising God and you know the church is far from dead! We've met so many people over the years who have credited the strength of their relationship with Jesus down to attending Soul Survivor during their teenage years, and it was a privilege for us to be able to share our story there.

While Mike was interviewing us one night during the main meeting he asked when we thought we would be able to start the village. I replied that I thought we would lay the first brick by the end of that year. This was in August and Joan gave me a talking to when we got off the stage. "How can you say that when we don't even have the land yet?" she asked. I couldn't explain it, it just felt right. That same evening we received a text from Murray saying he thought he'd found the right place for us.

We couldn't wait to get back to South Africa to see if it was the village I had pictured and the minute I set foot on the farm he had located I said, "This is it." We stood at the bottom of the hill and I could clearly see the long and winding road exactly as God had shown me. I could visualise the plantation, the sports field and the school all lining the road and leading up to a huge cross at the top of the hill, though at that stage it was all just overgrown grass and muddy paths. The farm was on the edge of Cottonlands, an informal settlement near Verulam, and we were warned that there was a lot of crime in the surrounding community, mainly due to the high unemployment, but I felt God say that wasn't a problem but an opportunity. That was why he told us to build the church first so that the very first thing we would be doing was sharing the love of Jesus with those who already lived there.

God had told me how much to pay for the land but when we were told the price this farm was being sold for it was almost twice as much. We offered the price God had given us and within two days we'd received a phone call to say the farm was ours. Due to some legal issues we were later offered the farm at R700,000 less (about £33,000/$49,000) but again, knowing God had said to pay the going rate, we stuck with our previous offer. Not everyone can understand that kind of decision and some thought I wasn't being a good steward, but I was trying to be obedient even when it didn't make sense to me. The land belonged to one of the community leaders and we later realised that if the community had seen us benefiting from the previous owner's misfortune they would never have trusted that our intentions were to bless and not to gain for ourselves. We were reminded once more that all God wants is our obedience even when it doesn't make sense.

As we stood looking at the empty fields where we imagined homes would be built and lives would be changed we couldn't quite believe the village we'd dreamt about so long ago was finally going to come to fruition. The grass was high and full of snakes and the only buildings were broken down chicken sheds and an old farmhouse that was in a terrible state. One thing I clearly remember Joan saying to me was, "Just don't ever ask me to move from my dream house on the beach and come and live here!" As a pair of city slickers, being on a farm would be our worst nightmare, and I promised her it would never happen.

WATOTO

Though God had given me a clear picture of the village we had no idea what to do next and needed a lot more information to help us prepare and work out how the village would actually run. We had used up our finances buying the land and so we said, "Now what, Lord?" I think this is exactly where God had wanted us to be: totally reliant on him. We heard about a couple called Gary and Marilyn Skinner who had planted a church in Uganda in 1984 and from there had started Watoto children's villages with exactly the same vision as us. They had three villages in different areas and were looking after around 3,000 children in total. Gary was speaking at a church nearby so we went to hear him and then spoke to him afterwards. He was excited by what God had been saying to us and invited us over to see it in action. Unfortunately, Joan got sick and couldn't make the first trip to Uganda so I went alone.

I was amazed at what I saw. It was a completed picture of the vision I had seen all those years ago. They had arranged the houses in circular clusters with a green space in the centre for the children to play. The homes were simple but well equipped, and each home had a foster mother and eight children. The mothers were themselves either widows or single and were often women who had been abused and who had found safety and purpose in being a foster mother. The village had all the essentials the children needed with a church right in the centre, a school, a medical centre, sports fields and a crèche for the pre-school children. God said, "This is my model, just follow it."

The thing that stirred my heart more than anything else was seeing how happy the children were. Of course there were times of tears and tantrums as in any family but they had such freedom and safety in the village and above all, they knew they were loved and cared for. The restoration of the family with Jesus Christ in the centre is truly God's plan for the orphaned children of our continent. We returned a number of times over the following years, taking others with us, to gain as much wisdom as we could from Gary and Marilyn who were so much further ahead in their journey than we were. They and their team were such a blessing to us as they freely shared their expertise and experiences and generously gave us their time as we asked hundreds of questions about what worked and what didn't and the ins and outs of running a village. What a blessing to see the success of these villages 20 years after they had begun.

We spent time with the children and chatted to the young people about what life was like for them in the village. We met one young lady who had come to Watoto at the age of seven and had received no education up to that point. Thanks to the input she had received, she was sitting before us as a graduate with a degree in agriculture and had returned to the village to run their agricultural programme. Her degree and her manner meant she would have been right at home in any corporate boardroom. It was a gift to us to see what she had achieved, inspiring us about the lives that could be turned around with the right environment.

Gary said God had told him he wanted 10,000 churches to build these villages across the continent, and he would use those children to change the face of Africa. He said they'd had many people come through their gates at Watoto excited about the idea of setting up a village but then nothing happened. His parting words were, "Tich, just go and do it!" and I left with that ringing in my ears and a determination in my heart to go and make it happen.

I was powerfully struck by how much had come from the one church that Gary and Marilyn had planted. They held five services every weekend in their main church in the city of Kampala, plus services in the other eight satellite venues for their over 20,000 members. They had birthed three children's villages and had created jobs for 2,000 vulnerable women. I asked God, "Why is this church making such a difference and impacting a nation?" He pointed me to a verse I knew well, James 1:27, which says, "Religion that God our Father accepts as pure and faultless is this: to look after orphans and widows in their distress and to keep oneself from being polluted by the world."

I had previously only ever focused on the first part of that verse as I grew in understanding about our role in looking after widows and orphans. Now I saw that there was also a call for us to rid ourselves of the world's pollution. If we go to church on a Sunday morning but don't let our relationship with Jesus impact our everyday lives, we will make no impact on the world. Even our churches are polluted by the world's standards, and we so easily gauge our success by the numbers of people attending, not by how much of an impact we're making in our communities. We think success is a big car, a big house, overseas holidays, often without giving a thought for the poor, whilst the Bible focuses much more on how we treat those who are in need.

Chapter 10

SHARING THE VISION

Jesus replied … "You give them something to eat." "We have here only five loaves of bread and two fish," they answered.

Matthew 14:16–17

Tich

We settled on a name for the village: Lungisisa Indlela Village (Zulu for "the right way" village), which we shortened to LIV, but we had no idea what to do next; all we had was a broken down chicken farm with no money to build even one house. God promised us he would bring the finances and the expertise and we were intrigued as to how he would provide. I had been selling insurance for many years and the first step God showed me was to use what was in my hands, that is, the talents and gifts he had given me. I knew I had to find 100 business people to give us R1,000 (£50/$70) each a month, which would help to fund the environmental and town planning applications and get us started.

He then told us to invite 4,000 people to a banquet at the International Convention Centre (ICC), bringing together the church, business and government, to share the vision and to raise the money we needed. We couldn't imagine how we could pull off a banquet on that scale. People talk about being at the end of their rope, well we felt like we were at the end of a rope that was hanging over the edge of a cliff. We were completely out of our depth and all we could say to God was, "We're letting go; this is yours to do with as you will."

The first miracle came in the form of a pair of helping hands. A friend, Karin, came to visit; she had returned from working as an au pair overseas. We knew she was a good organiser and asked if she could help us while she was looking for a job. We explained the position we were in and that we could only give her a small amount of money but as we mentioned the figure her eyes widened. Excitedly she told us, "As I was driving here God told me I was going to be offered that exact amount of money for a job and that I was to take it!" It was our first glimpse of how God was going to help us pull off the banquet.

We had a group of faithful ladies who were praying for us and one said, "When God has a special event, he always has a specific date," so we started to pray about what that date might be. A few weeks later another lady said she felt like Jesus was saying he would pass over the event. Passover! That was the time for the banquet. So we looked up the Passover date for the following year. The Passover feast in 2010 would be held on 6th April, and when we asked the ICC for their availability for that year they had just four dates free. Two were in February and the others were the 6th and 7th of April!

We phoned back to book the 6th and were told that this date was no longer available, only the 7th. We were disheartened as this wasn't the exact date of Passover. Without knowing this, one of our prayer ladies shared that she'd been listening to some teaching from a Messianic Jew about the feasts. He had said that the new day Jesus was ushering in comes the day *after* the Passover meal. God intended all along for the banquet to be on the 7th! Once more God confirmed to us that this was his plan. I suspect he was also having some fun with us as he gave us these clues to follow.

The next challenge was how to pay for the banquet which was going to cost R1.7 million (£80,000/$120,000). With 50 per cent of the fee needed up front there was only one option: we had to take out a mortgage on our house. We hadn't at that point sold one table, however we felt at peace that this was God's plan and we trusted him as we took this giant step. It was one of those times when you just know that he's in it and everything will be OK.

People said it would be impossible to get 4,000 people together on a weekday evening, especially to hear about orphan children. We had to choose to trust what we believed God was showing us, and leading up to the event we kept reminding him that this was *his* banquet, especially when the doubt and panic rose up within us!

We were given two bits of advice from Christians: we shouldn't mention the name of Jesus if we wanted to raise money and we shouldn't waste our time with government. As we prayed for the banquet I felt God say, "Tell them about me." I was reminded again of the original vision to bring government, business and the church together. I also knew you couldn't look after orphaned and vulnerable children without partnering with government and I had to be obedient to what God had said.

A GOD CONNECTION

A month before the banquet, we still hadn't made contact with anyone from government. Then, one of our contacts gave us the personal mobile phone number of the KwaZulu-Natal Premier Dr. Zweli Mkhize, telling us we should go directly to him as he had the same passion for the children and would love the vision. With nothing to lose I called him that night. I was amazed he answered the phone and listened to what I had to say as I quickly shared the vision and asked if I could meet with him. He later told Joan that he never answers his phone but that night he did and "there was this white man on the other end of the line who said his name was 'Tich'. He was talking so fast about orphans and widows I could hardly understand what he was saying and I was still stuck on his name thinking, *What kind of a name is Tich?* But I heard his heart and told him to come and see me the next week."

I walked in to Dr. Mkhize's office the following Monday armed with my architect's impression of what the village would look like, and we had the most amazing meeting. I told him the vision and shared my heart. Dr. Mkhize told me the fact that we had bought the land with our own money showed him that this was going to happen with or without their help, so it was best that they be a part of it. I said we couldn't partner with government if they wanted a say in the running of the village, as Jesus had to be the centre of LIV and it needed to be run by the church on biblical principles. The Bible doesn't say that government must look after the widows and orphans; it clearly states that the church needs to look after them. I went on to tell him that neither he nor the president of South Africa had the answer to these problems in our country but there's only one person who had the answer and that's Jesus Christ.

Dr. Mkhize's PA was taking notes and her eyes nearly popped out of her head at the boldness of my words but Dr. Mkhize simply said, "Tich, I agree with you 100 per cent." He said he would come and speak at our banquet and he would bring ministers, members of the executive council and heads of departments. I couldn't believe it! God had opened the door to us working with government just as he'd promised. It was the start of a wonderful relationship and Dr. Mkhize and his wife, Dr. May, have been such a blessing to us as they share our heart and passion for the vulnerable and orphaned children of our nation.

DON'T TAKE THE GLORY

Tich and Joan

As we were preparing for the banquet God gave us two pictures via ladies who were praying for us. The first was represented by a hand being drawn across the throat in a cutting motion. We knew this was a clear reminder that we were not to take any of the glory. We mustn't get puffed up and think that we were something special because we were putting on a huge banquet or gaining the ear of government. God doesn't share his glory; everything we have is his and everything we do must be to bring him glory, not to make ourselves look good.

He is the one who opens doors for us to walk through. The other picture was of us driving through farmland where there were no street lights. It was a cloudy night with no stars and all we could see was the ground that the car's lights illuminated ahead. God was telling us that this was all he was going to show us, that he knew the destination we were heading to and we needed to trust him completely every step of the way. He continues to challenge us: "Will you go where you don't know you are going, knowing that I know where you are going?"

FEEDING OF THE 4,000

Joan

When Tich first told me we needed to have a banquet for 4,000 people I reminded him that 2,000 for breakfast nearly wiped us out! Not being a cook I couldn't imagine feeding so many. "How do we feed so many people, God?" I asked. A foolish question to ask a God who only needed two fish and five loaves of bread! The ICC said that they had never hosted a dinner for 4,000 people before, but they believed it was doable. However, no event coordinator was prepared to take on something they saw as so risky. We had no choice but to do it ourselves with a team of women from the church.

God is always in the detail and he led us every step of the way, even showing us what he wanted at the centre of each table. We couldn't have candles as these would be a fire hazard, and to have beautiful flowers for 400 tables would have cost us a fortune. One elderly lady, Merle, from our church drew a picture on a napkin of a beautiful multicoloured beaded cross. We found a Zimbabwean street trader who handmade each one and we put lights underneath them to light up on the night. It was a sight to behold.

The logistics of feeding 4,000 people are huge! The hall was the size of two and a half rugby fields lying end to end. We almost needed roller skates to get from one end to the other! We had nine huge screens, placed at regular intervals, so everyone could see what was happening on the stage. There were 44 buffet stations—each double-sided to make sure everyone was served quickly. The night before the banquet a group who prayed for the city came to pray over each area of the hall. They told me that some of the decor on the buffet tables that had been provided by the ICC were items with demonic connotations. They asked what they should do and I panicked. If we removed them the stations would be bare and would look terrible, ruining all the hard work we'd put in to make the rest of the room look welcoming. "Could you remove the really bad stuff and just pray over the rest?" I said.

A moment later I realised how ridiculous that was. This was God's banquet and there could be nothing in the room that didn't honour him so I ran after the team and asked them to take the whole lot down. Amazingly we had made extra beaded crosses and there were just enough for each station to have one. The stations looked perfect! How easy it is as believers to compromise if we aren't alert.

We had our LIV logo designed and used all the beautiful, bright colours it contains to colour-code the arrival and seating areas, matching the different coloured tablecloths so that people could easily find where they were going and wouldn't have to hike from one end of the room to the other to get to the right spot. We even colour-coded the waistcoats worn by the hosts for each section so everything was clear, and many commented on the level of excellence and detail and how smoothly everything ran.

Tich

For six months I met with church leaders and business men and women to get them to buy tables. The response was overwhelming, and with the 13 tables the Premier had booked, I realised that the part of the vision that God had given me 13 years earlier to bring business, government and the church together had been fulfilled.

It was an incredible evening. The Watoto choir who came from Uganda to perform were amazing; Peter Pollock opened in prayer; Rory Dyer, a well-known young charismatic Christian leader who has made an impact in the business and church world, shared about the Father heart of God; Dr. Mkhize spoke about the importance of government, business and the church working together to tackle one of our biggest problems; and I shared the God-given vision for the village. Shaun Pollock (Peter's son, and himself a former South African cricket captain), was the MC for the evening, along with John Smit, a former World Cup-winning rugby captain.

It was a memorable evening, enjoyed by all. We had people from every colour and creed, showing them respect as we catered for their dietary requirements, including halal and kosher food. Nobody was offended as we shared what we believed to be God's vision for the children of our nation, and many pledged their support that evening.

It was a reminder we must not be ashamed of the gospel; it is time for us as believers to confess Christ to the nations.

The banquet was the catapult that put LIV in the forefront of the minds of many and unlocked the funding we needed to build the village, just as God had shown us. God had done more than we could ever have believed or dared to imagine.

Chapter 11

CLOSING THE GAP

Whatever you did for one of the least of these
brothers and sisters of mine, you did for me.
Matthew 25:40

Tich

When we bought the farm we assumed that we would be able to plug into the main municipal sewerage system. There was only one problem: we discovered there was no municipal sewerage line to the area! It's understandable that whilst lots of companies like to sponsor children and build houses, nobody wants to put their name to a sewer so I went to the Premier for help. He said he couldn't give us the money, but he could open the door for me to go to the cabinet as the ministers of the different government departments had their own budgets. If they felt that what we were doing was a solution to the orphan problem, they would be able to release funds. He invited me to speak at a cabinet meeting at Pietermaritzburg and to share the vision, a hugely daunting moment for someone who had no experience in the political arena. After I spoke the Minister for Health addressed the room. He said he'd just returned from Rwanda where he'd seen babies feeding off the breasts of their dead mothers. He said, "We are fast going down the same road unless we do something about it. After what we've seen and heard today in cabinet how can we as the government stand in the way of God's vision for the children of this nation?"

The following week I received a memo to say that each of the 13 government departments was on board. Together they pledged enough money to help us with the sewerage as well as other key infrastructure, such as roads, fencing and electricity; they funded the building of a multi-purpose village hall, sports facilities and an early childhood development centre for 200 children. They gave us the money and support to develop agricultural land and the city municipality gave us funds to build a clothing factory that would not only train and employ local people, but would provide a means of income for the village. Most importantly they gave us money to build 96 three-bedroomed houses that would be home to up to 700 children. It was astonishing.

The Premier gave me a letter that opened many doors, encouraging business, government and the church to partner with us in our endeavour to provide holistic residential care for widows, orphans and vulnerable children where they would be raised up in a Christian environment using biblical principles.[1] I asked him whether a letter stating that we were bringing up the children in a

---

1   See Appendix 2 for a copy of the letter.

Christian environment, written on the Premier's letterhead, would cause trouble for him. He answered, "This is a country of free choice. If you don't want Jesus, you don't have to go to this village, but you can't object to the way someone else believes is the best way to bring up these children. If another religious group came to me with a project that I thought would work, as a politician I would consider it." We are very proud of our democracy having seen that in many so-called "free" countries, Christians don't have the freedom to openly express their belief.

Now we were beginning to understand why God had told me to bring government, business and the church together. It is vital for us to work together considering the scale of our orphan problem as none of us can do it alone. We began to see God's plan coming together: the government has the capital needed to build the village, the church has the heart to love and nurture broken lives, and businesses can provide the finances to support ongoing costs. If we work together I truly believe we can put a roof over every vulnerable and orphaned child's head, give them a mother to love them, feed and educate them, to the glory of God. If we do that, our nation will be changed forever.

A NEW ZONE

Before we could start building we needed to get permission to change the usage of the land. My brother advised me that it can take up to three years for land to be rezoned so we were prepared for a drawn out process. I filled in the application forms saying we wanted to build residential houses, a school, a church, a shop and a clothing factory, whilst using further land for farming. In reply I received a phone call from the minister's office saying that our plans covered the residential, educational, religious, agricultural, commercial, industrial and retail sectors on one plot of land, and they didn't have a zoning category that could cover it. However, the woman on the phone said she would deal with the application personally, and within seven days we had the approval. They had created a new zoning for the village. We believe this not only opened the door for our village to be built but provided a prototype for villages to be built all over the nation. Only God could have opened these doors and poured out so much favour. He had fast-tracked the vision and the funding and the building of the village began.

Working with government was new to me and it was a learning curve to deal with their busy schedules that meant meetings were frequently postponed or cancelled at the last minute, or I'd receive phone calls saying I needed to come in right away. With my focus full-time on the village I was able to be flexible and that enabled me to nurture the amazing relationships with provincial and national government that are now such a huge blessing to us in our work.

BUSINESS AND JOB CREATION

Tich and Joan

As well as working with government, one of the other parts of the vision that had confused us was how taking care of children and job creation were linked. One of the biggest problems in our nation is the unacceptably high rate of unemployment which has led to possibly the biggest problem we face: the disparity between the rich and poor. We had no idea how caring for orphans could enable us to create jobs for others in the community.

As plans for the village began to unfold, however, and we started to build the houses, the school, the healthcare centre and the hall, we realised we were able to employ more than 100 labourers, bricklayers and plasterers. We could see that as the village developed there would be further opportunities for full-time employment as we would need cleaners, people to work in the fields to help us grow our own vegetables, grass cutters, and a maintenance team for the buildings. We soon started to see that God was giving us a vision of how his church could significantly help to close the gap. By training and upskilling people and ultimately creating and finding employment for them we can give them the opportunity to sustain their families. Giving someone a job so they can afford to feed their family is far more honouring and beneficial in the long term than giving a handout.

We also wanted to create a number of businesses that would plough their profits back into the village to eventually make it self-sustainable. We already had an inkling this might be one of many villages God wanted to create over the years to come in order to look after the millions of orphaned and vulnerable children in our country. We also knew that these villages couldn't be funded on donations alone. We needed to start thinking about a range of products that people would buy for their excellence, not because they wanted to help out LIV as a charity. Our initial ideas were for a clothing factory, given Joan's experience in that area, and a cut flower business. We didn't fully know or understand God's plan but we could already see that we needed to trust him that bringing the church, government and business together was the way to make LIV work.

Chapter 12

THE VILLAGE OPENS

Love never fails.

1 Corinthians 13:8

HAND-PICKING THE MOTHERS

Tich and Joan

Whilst all the building work was going on there was another hugely important piece of the puzzle: finding the right mothers to look after the children and love them like their own. Each house is designed to take up to eight children, so each mother can look after up to six foster children as well as having the option of having one or two of her own biological children under the age of 12 with her too.[1] We knew these mothers would need to be very special women indeed.

---

[1] Mothers with young teenage children are advised that it's not the best season for them to be in the village so they can concentrate on their own family until their children have left home.

We spoke to pastors from local churches around the city and in rural communities to ask them to gather groups of women that they thought would be both suitable and interested and we shared the vision with them. We spoke with thousands of women, knowing we had to spread the net wide to find the right people. Being a mother in the village is so much more than just a job; we were seeking those who felt a strong sense of calling to look after orphaned and vulnerable children and who were willing to make a lifelong commitment to God, to the village and to these children.

We didn't want women who would come for a short season or those who simply saw it as a way of getting a safe home for themselves and food on the table. We needed women who would spend the rest of their lives loving and serving the children in their LIV family, providing the same security and love as any healthy blood-related family. Our heart and the vision was that we would create a true family, a safe place, a place of belonging where they would receive healing and wholeness.

In institutions fostered children are on their own once they turn 18, whereas we wanted to provide a supportive and loving environment for each child for the rest of their lives. We knew it was important to not only help them through their childhood but also through any further education and training to enable them to establish themselves as young adults, able to support and sustain themselves and their future families. As with any caring family, your children only leave home when they are able to get a job and fend for themselves. It is vital for us that the mothers we employ will recognise and hone their adopted/fostered children's gifts and talents, and guide them into being able to earn a living and become positive role models for future generations.

MODELLING THE FATHER HEART

We are often asked where the fathers are, and why we don't have couples in the homes. In an ideal world we would have, but it's very difficult to find married couples who are willing to make the sacrifices it takes to parent in the village. We saw from the Watoto model that it was key to teach into the Father heart of God so each child knows they have a Father in heaven who loves them. We also saw it was important to have men of good character living and working in the village who would be role models and could help the mothers with discipline where required.

Our commitment to the mothers is as strong as it is to the children. It was always our heart to work with these women, helping them grow and develop their skills and gifts and be all that they could be. During the training sessions we asked the mothers what dreams they had when they were younger that hadn't been fulfilled, and they invariably said they wanted to be nurses, social workers or teachers. These dreams had stalled for many reasons in their lives, but now they were being given the opportunity to use these nurturing skills in a new way at LIV.

Ann, who had worked with us in Amaoti, did all the recruiting and preparation, including personal development of the potential mothers before they came to the village. Some had come from broken and abusive backgrounds themselves, or had been widowed or abandoned by the men in their lives. Ann would help them lean on God and allow him to heal their past hurts and deal with unforgiveness and disappointments. We wanted them to be as free as possible for their own sakes, but also so that they could love the children placed in their care from a place of wholeness.

We have found over the years that many are interested in the vision but after the final two weeks of intensive, full-time training only a few go on to become registered as LIV mothers. Anyone who is tempted by the idea of the security that the village offers soon discovers that they will never last. Looking after children who have been traumatised and been through much pain and suffering in their short lives is tough. The children are often damaged by the things that they have witnessed and experienced, and so their behaviour reflects the pain and confusion that runs deep. Mothers in the village need deep wells of love to be able to draw from. The selection process is rigorous so that we end up with a team of hand-picked, special women who make wonderful mothers to the children of LIV.

THE FIRST FAMILIES

Our next step was to find the right couple to manage the village and the church.

We felt strongly that Elliott and Dolly Sonjica, who were elders at one of our local churches and had planted a number of churches over the years, were the perfect couple. We had approached them with the idea when we first bought the land but the timing wasn't right for them. However, when we met up again a year later they were ready, and agreed to move onto the village with their two children, Grace and Elijah.

It made sense for them to live in the farmhouse that was placed right at the centre of the village, but it was falling to pieces and in desperate need of some renovations. We didn't want to cut corners on their house and felt like we should fix it up as though it was where we were going to live ourselves. It was in a terrible mess: tiles were falling off the roof and the ceilings were crumbling; the kitchen had a rusted sink, chipped wall tiles, and dark wooden storage cupboards that were falling apart. The floors were covered in so much grime that we didn't know they were wooden until we began cleaning them. There wasn't even a bathroom to speak of. But slowly that disused and unloved building became a beautiful farmhouse with a black and white tiled kitchen floor, polished wooden floorboards, new kitchen and bathroom units, a flower and vegetable garden at the front, and a wonderful homely feel.

Overgrown land around the farm was cleared, along with black mambas, spitting cobras and puff adders, and we turned one of the old chicken sheds into a church hall. As we had no money for windows or doors it was little more than four walls and a floor but it was a start. We had raised funds for the first cluster of houses, and the building of these homes began; each one was painted red, with splashes of other bright colours on the doors and windows. The homes were simple but welcoming, placed in clusters around grassed areas where children could play.

On 9th August 2011 the first six mothers moved on to the village. It seemed appropriate that the date the village began was South Africa's National Women's Day.[2] The sun shone and we were all filled with hope and excitement as God's vision became a reality. The LIV school started the following week in one of the houses with six of the mothers' own children, run by two volunteer teachers. LIV was

---

2   In South Africa, Women's Day is a public holiday, and women are celebrated during the whole month of August.

registered as a residential long-term cluster foster care village and social welfare departments began to place children with us. It can be a lengthy process as each case goes through the courts but soon our new children began to arrive. It is hard to express how we all felt as we welcomed our new LIV family members. The mothers said it was like being pregnant as they waited for the arrival of their God-given children.

We were deeply saddened when a social worker who brought a child to LIV told us we shouldn't get too emotionally involved in the children's lives. This was the opposite to God's vision to love these children as our own. Although we understand why in human terms this attitude makes sense, it is one of the biggest reasons why the foster system fails children in so many countries around the world.

STRETCHED BEYOND OUR LIMITS

As we worked with social services to bring more children to the village we told them to give us the children that no one else wanted, and we began to realise the horror of what these little ones had been through. Some were traumatised from witnessing the deaths of loved ones, many because of AIDS. Others had been abused both physically and sexually by the adults who should have loved and protected them, and so were unsurprisingly distrustful of adults. Some had seen violence that no child, or even adult, should ever be a witness to. Many children had been neglected and some were found living on the streets. Sometimes the children wouldn't even sleep in a bed; they were so used to sleeping outside that they would rather sleep on the veranda of the house.

We realised the children needed to be taught everything from how to sit and eat dinner as a family, to how to treat one another with love and respect. School was alien to many which impacted everything from their ability to sit in a chair during lessons to their delayed education and understanding, and that meant we had to set careful, tailor-made curricula to meet their needs. The trauma they had experienced was often evident in their behaviour. People say that those who have been abused often go on to abuse others, and we could see we needed to stop these cycles of harmful behaviour and rather bring healing and wholeness.

All of these challenges stretched us far beyond our limits and very quickly we were hit with the reality of what we were doing. "Help, God!" we cried out, brought to our knees with the realisation that we were so unqualified to help these children. God kept reminding us that love never fails, and that he was rescuing these children and taking them from darkness to light. All we had to give was his love, so we would speak positive words over each child, hugging them and telling them again and again how wonderful and beautiful they are in the sight of God and that he had a plan and purpose for their lives. We watched in awe as these children changed before our eyes as we loved them with the love of Christ.

Over time we have added social workers, psychologists, counsellors and occupational therapists to the team who help the children process their trauma and deal with it in an effective way. We want to care for these children in every way possible and that includes looking after their emotional and spiritual health. Ultimately true wholeness only comes through the Holy Spirit; anyone can build a village but only Jesus and the love of Christ at work through us can transform lives.

OVERCOMING MISTRUST

Joan

We also hit another big bump in the road. When we had asked the first mothers to join us we hadn't been in a position to give them any kind of income; we just provided their housing and food. After a few months we wanted to give them something they could spend on themselves and we were able to give them a small allowance. Over time we were able to increase this amount as sponsorships came in, which gave the mothers opportunity to help their extended families outside of the village. We didn't think anything of it but our board told us that if someone is reliant on you for more than 70 per cent of their livelihood, they are deemed to be employees and have to have a contract. We wrestled over this as we knew the hearts of the mothers and that they were doing this for the Lord and not for personal gain and that they would find the idea of turning that into a legal contract a hard thing to take. We approached them with heavy hearts and they felt betrayed and as though we were imposing a set of rules on them because we didn't trust them. They adamantly wanted to remain as volunteers and so we were stuck.

I asked for a meeting with them, Elliot and Dolly, and we sat together to try and find a way forward. I could see the mistrust in the mothers' eyes towards me and the offence they were feeling. We all have our default buttons in times of difficulty and here in South Africa so often our default is the legacy we've inherited from the apartheid era—a legacy of mistrust across the races. I could completely understand that they didn't trust me; they had been subjected to so much by white people who had tried to reduce them to second class citizens. We talked and we talked but there came a point that I realised no amount of words would help. I prayed that God would help me break the deadlock and show the women I loved them. Immediately I sensed what he wanted me to do. Without saying a word I got up, filled a bowl of water and fetched a towel and soap. Then one by one I knelt before each mother and washed her feet.

It was a moment I will never forget. Where words had failed, God came in and broke down the barriers dividing us. As I washed their feet we all wept and God's perfect love flooded us. I felt despair and anguish welling up within me for what we as whites had done. The atmosphere changed in the room that day as his grace overwhelmed us, and as our masks came off we began to knit together like a true family. The mothers became like our daughters, and the children quickly began to call us Baba (which means Father) and Gogo (which means Granny).

When we had the vision we saw a heavenly place with kids laughing, happy and grateful. We hadn't thought about how many tears there would be. We soon realised the village would be like any other family that has its ups and downs, its highs and lows. Tears as well as laughter are the sounds of life and so we embrace the good and the bad, knowing we face them together.

JJ'S AND SLI'S STORY

Tich

For the vast majority of the children, we don't meet their parents, families or carers before they come to the village, but Sli is different.

Her father, JJ, lived on the streets of Umhlanga Rocks, the village where our beach house is, and we met him when he was a young teenager. He was clearly a born leader and was head of the gang of street kids he spent all of his time with. I used to make sandwiches for them and they would congregate at our offices each week where I would talk to them about Jesus. JJ had a wonderful sense of humour and in his own brash way we could see he really cared for the younger boys.

Mike Pilavachi and a team from Soul Survivor also connected with JJ and the "Umhlanga Boys" and were investing in their lives. They raised funds in the UK to buy a house where the boys could live, and sent a young lady called Becca who had completed a PhD looking specifically at the laws in South Africa in relation to street children, to be their "house mother". By this time these young boys had become older teenagers and some were even hardened criminals. Mike and Becca could see that putting them into a house with Becca as their "mother" would not be a safe option for her, so she continued to work with them on the streets.

Things became very difficult and Becca returned to the UK, so Mike asked us to keep an eye on JJ and the others. One late afternoon I went to meet with them and found JJ hitting Zandile, a prostitute, over the head with a brick. I rushed to separate them with the help of some of the other boys but JJ picked up a broken bottle and came for me. He was clearly under the influence of drugs and out of his mind, and I fled for my life, jumped in my car and returned home, shaken to the core.

The next day I felt God wanted me to go back. I found JJ sitting in the gutter with his head in his hands. It was a major turning point in our relationship as he couldn't believe I would come back after what he had tried to do. He asked me, "Please, Ticher, take me off the streets and help me get off the drugs." Mike agreed to use some of the funds they had raised, and we managed to get JJ into a drug rehabilitation centre.

We visited him regularly over the next three months. He recommitted his life to Jesus, and during one of my visits confessed to me that he was struggling to sleep, and was riddled with guilt and full of fear as he had once accidentally killed a man; he didn't think God could really forgive him. We prayed together on a bench under a tree that day and asked his heavenly Father to forgive him, cleanse him with the blood of Jesus, and deliver him from the guilt and fear. Mike also came with us during one of our visits and JJ confessed to him that every time he saw Mike and his team, he would ask them to buy shoes as this was the easiest item for them to sell to buy drugs. Mike was mortified to think he may have aided and perpetuated their drug habit! The reality is they would have just robbed someone else to get the drugs, they were so heavily addicted.

Three months later, the rehab centre called to say that JJ was ready to be discharged. We knew if he went back onto the streets it would be only a matter of time before he was back to his old ways so Joan wisely said we needed to take him into our home. He came to live with us and we will never forget the six months he stayed. JJ very quickly slotted into family life, though we had to teach him everything from scratch, including how to eat with a knife and fork at a table, and even how to use a toilet. He was horrified at the salads and vegetables we gave him to eat, and convinced Nora, our domestic worker, to cook him separate meals of mielie (maize), beans and samp (rice), the staple African diet. There was never a dull moment!

JJ reconnected with his uncle, brother and sister, who lived in Stanger, an hour's drive from Umlhanga, and we also got his friends Nicky and Zandile, the prostitute, into rehab with the support of Soul Survivor. The change in them, too, was remarkable. Zandile became an amazing evangelist and continued to share the love of Jesus with others until she died from the AIDS virus a few years later. We found JJ and Nicky a place to stay in Amaoti, and they ran the Lungisani Indlela donations store. Probably not the most appropriate job for them as we noticed that every month they were wearing new shoes taken from the donations they were supposed to be distributing to the Amaoti community!

We often spoke to them about the AIDS virus and encouraged them to get tested as we could see that they were both getting thinner, a sure sign of the disease. JJ always said he was too afraid of needles and hospitals and refused to be tested. One day, we got a call from Nicky to say JJ was dying. We took him to the clinic and the prognosis wasn't good. He had tuberculosis, a side effect of the virus, and was wasting away. He could hardly walk. The doctors could do no more for him as it was too late to put him onto the AIDS treatment. JJ went back to his family in Stanger, where they looked after him.

A short while after he went home, one of the street girls arrived at our house with a four-day-old baby girl in her arms. "JJ told me you'd help me," she said, and we soon realised the baby, Sli, was JJ's daughter! We took her to visit JJ and he was so very proud and asked us to take care of her. He died just a few days later.

Sli is now four years old and lives in the village with her two younger brothers and a LIV foster mother. Her birth mother came to live with Sli at first and we tried to teach her to be a cleaner. Sadly, she chose to go back to the streets; it's a hard life but it is what she knows. In the years since she has brought us other children she has given birth to. We try to get her to use preventative methods but she chooses her own way and she is now pregnant with her fourth child.

Every time we look at Sli we see JJ. She is his mirror image! What we were unable to do for her father and mother we know we are able to give to her and her siblings: hope and a future to develop their God-given talents.

We will never forget JJ and our journey with him. We know he is in heaven where he has finally found home. *Humba Khahle*, JJ, our son ("Go well, JJ"), until we meet again.

Chapter 13

WHO'S IN CHARGE?

Unless the LORD builds the house, the builders labour in vain.

Psalm 127:1

GOD PICKS THE TEAM

Tich and Joan

When LIV started, the staff team was just the two of us working from an office in our home. We knew we were completely out of our depth but God promised us that he would bring us the finances and expertise we needed. The very first person who supported us financially was a young lady from the UK by the name of Rhiannon, whom we had never met. She heard about LIV and felt God ask her to give us her savings of £5,000 ($7,000). We were blown away by her generosity and hugely encouraged at God's provision. Offers of help started to come in too and we began to see miracle after miracle.

Early on we tried to give God a helping hand in finding the right staff until God said, "Are you picking the team or am I?" He told us very clearly that we had two choices: we could do our plans in which case we would need to pay for them, or we could do things his way and he would take care of all of our needs. We knew his plans were better than ours and that he definitely has more money than we do so we figured it would be best to follow his plans!

We have seen God provide people in the most amazing ways. When we were just starting, two teachers from Canada and Norway volunteered their services, and so we were able to school our first children. Whilst we were praying for a PA we were invited to share the vision for LIV at Glenridge Church in the city and at the end a heavily pregnant lady called Mandy waddled up and said she'd love to volunteer. She was the perfect PA for us, as well as having experience in running events, and we immediately employed her. People said no one in their right mind would offer a job to a heavily pregnant woman, but we knew she was the person God had brought along for us. We soon had a team of volunteers and staff, including a much-needed bookkeeper. Ann, who had worked with us in Amaoti, agreed to come and work with us too and was an invaluable help to us, the mothers, and the growing team.

André is a wonderful paediatrician who was invited to our banquet by some friends. He didn't want to go as he hated having to dress up and be in crowded rooms, and when he got near the ICC and saw the amount of people waiting to park, he almost headed home. Thankfully his wife, Ilse, was having none of it and by the end of the evening he felt God nudging him to get on board and use his skills to make a difference. He gave up much of his spare time to care for our children's medical needs, which was such a blessing to us, but as the number of children in the village grew, this arrangement became unmanageable and we knew we were going to need someone full-time. We prayed for a doctor though we knew we didn't have the budget to be able to pay for one.

One Saturday morning we had a meeting with André and the nurses about the way forward, and a lady called Gerlinde joined us. We thought André had brought her along and he thought that we had. At the end of the meeting we asked what her story was and she said she was running an intensive care unit in a central London hospital. Some weeks previously the LIV logo had popped up on her computer and she couldn't get rid of it. Eventually she clicked to see what it was, found our website and heard God say she was to come.

Gerlinde told God she was very happy where she was. Though she had been born in South Africa she had been living in London for 21 years and was very settled. However, she had already planned to come back to visit her mother and decided while she was here she would pop into the village and see what we were doing. She envisaged that we wouldn't be in need of a doctor and she would be able to say she had explored the possibility and then could return to London with a clear conscience. Instead we told her we had been praying for her to come. "This is the weirdest job interview I've ever experienced," she replied.

We took her for a walk around the village and explained we couldn't offer very much money. "Don't worry," she said. "Whatever you're able to give me is fine." Our offer was roughly a tenth of the salary she was earning, but she went back to London and handed in her resignation, much to the confusion of her bosses. They thought she'd lost her mind to be giving up a prestigious London job with so many perks to work for a tiny salary on the middle of some old farmland in Durban, but God had called her. What seemed like foolishness to others was God at work in her life, and within three months of our meeting she had sold her car and all her possessions and arrived in the village ready to work and look after our children.

Another time we were praying for someone to help with our finances. Months went by with seemingly no answer to our cries. Our accountant was about to leave and we were getting desperate. Unbeknown to us, a wonderful woman called Louise was feeling God stirring her to give up her job as a financial manager of a big company. She thought perhaps he would call her to a charity like UNICEF or World Vision. She was at a conference when she heard us sharing about LIV and as we played our video about the village she felt God say, "That's where I want you to go." She obediently resigned and shortly afterwards arrived at LIV, dropping around two thirds of her salary in the process. Her old boss tried to convince her to come back, offering double her salary, but she was sold out for God and his vision for the children, saying, "You don't understand; no amount of money can buy what I have here at LIV."

Athi was working for a commercial underwriter when God started to speak to her about the poverty in her community. She knew that parents left their children at 4 a.m. when they went to work with no one to look after them, and it started to break her heart. She was at a braai[1] when one of our volunteers told her we were looking for a PA, so she came to meet with us. By the time the

---

1   A barbecue.

appointment came round we'd already found someone, but we spoke anyway and there was a deep connection so we invited her to come and be part of the marketing team.

When her husband, Chester, picked her up we got chatting and discovered that he had come to Durban to play rugby for the Sharks.[2] He had represented South Africa with the under-19 side and captained the Sharks under-20s, but in 2006 he had broken a bone in his foot, effectively ending his rugby-playing career. He had started coaching at the Sharks Academy and was known to be a man of great sporting talent and integrity. As soon as we heard his story and saw his passion for God and his love for children, we offered him a job as our director of sport. We had a feeling both Chester and Athi would be key people in the future of LIV.

Every single person who comes to LIV has a miraculous story to tell of how they got here and how God called them. We've learned that when we try and find staff we often get it wrong but when we trust and pray, we see him provide in the most amazing ways. He has spoken to so many people and drawn them to LIV in ways that we never could.

God has also provided us with so much support and so many amazing ambassadors who have shared about LIV around the world. Two South African captains, John Smit and Shaun Pollock, have both made themselves available to us as much as they can, attending functions and helping us with fundraising. John even donated the money towards our sports field where the young people train. Another ambassador who we are very proud of is our son, Grant

2   The KwaZulu Natal provincial (state) rugby team.

(Twiggy) Baker, who is a world renowned big wave surfer, crowned world number one in the sport in 2014. He is passionate about the village and what we are doing, and wherever he goes he promotes LIV. Another faithful ambassador is David Miller, one of South Africa's top limited overs cricketers who is seldom seen without his LIV wristband.

Many more leading sportsmen from KwaZulu-Natal, South Africa and overseas have proudly worn their wristbands to help create awareness. The UK rugby team Saracens wore the LIV logo on their jerseys for a season, and played a practice match in the village against College Rovers during their pre-season tour. We see a great humility in all these guys and a desire to help those who are less fortunate, and we're so grateful for their support.

Chapter 14

WILL YOU GO?

All the believers were together and had everything in common. They sold property and possessions to give to anyone who had need.

Acts 2:44–45

Joan

Fifteen months after the first family had moved on to LIV, Elliot and Dolly, who had been overseeing both the church and the village, dropped the bombshell that they felt it was time for them to move on. We had thought they would be there for many more years so were shocked, but started to pray and ask God who he would send to step into their shoes. There was silence. The more we prayed, the heavier the silence seemed. Then Tich came to me and said, "I think God wants us to move on to the village." "That's fine," I replied, "I'll help you pack and I'll come and visit on weekends!"

I had no intention of moving out of our beautiful beach house. It had been home for so many years and as much as I loved the village, I couldn't imagine living there full-time. Living by the sea had always been my dream; not to mention the fact that the main bedroom at the farmhouse was the same size as our bathroom at the beach house.

At the time I was reading a book a friend had given me by Michele Perry, called *Love Has a Face*. Michelle is an American who has one leg and one hip, but that didn't stop her from following God's call to go to war-torn Southern Sudan to open a home for orphaned children. I woke up one morning laughing and said to Tich, "I'd better say yes to going to Cottonlands before God sends me to Southern Sudan!"

It honestly had never entered our minds that we would live in the village, but God in his grace was doing as he promised and only showing us one step at a time; the whole picture would have been far more than we could have handled.

On 7th December 2012 we packed up the last of our things and left our beach house. I can vividly remember driving towards the village, my back seat piled high with our belongings, and hearing God's audible voice say, "That's no longer your home; the farmhouse in the village is now your home." It was a shock, and as I was processing it a huge thunderstorm began. As I turned into the road LIV is on, the storm stopped as suddenly as it had begun. It felt like the rain had performed a spiritual and physical cleansing. I'd been given a word that I was pregnant with the village and it seemed as though the rain also signified the waters breaking.

We weren't ready to sell the beach house, but shortly after we moved a company came and offered to rent it for a year and we knew it was God. He was helping us to sever our ties to our old home so we could fully embrace the new one. We had to take out all of our personal effects including paintings, photographs and some pieces of furniture and bring them to the farmhouse. This made our new house more like our home and we knew this was part of God's plan. One thing we couldn't take with us was the air conditioning, and oh how we missed it as the summer temperatures spiked and the heat stifled us. None of the other homes in the village have air con so we didn't think it would be right for us to have it either. We decided not to bring our TV with us and managed to live without it for seven months until Wimbledon and the British Open were about to start and then we caved in and bought one!

The farmhouse was very different from our beach house but we settled in and were thankful that God had prompted us to fix it up for Elliot and Dolly as though we were going to live in it ourselves! But three days after our move I was asking God, "What am I doing here?" Tich had taken to village life like a fish to water but I couldn't see my place or what value I was going to add by living in the village.

That afternoon I was sitting on the couch showing a volunteer English doctor pictures of how the farmhouse had looked when we bought the land and one of the little girls from the village came in. We had told everyone that our home was open to them 24-7 and wanted them to know they were welcome in our house at any time in the same way any grandparent opens their home to their grandchildren. The little girl came and sat down next to me; she didn't say a word, just sat by my side as we looked

at the photos. A few more children came in and they began playing together, jumping on the black and white square tiles in the
kitchen. When they went outside I followed them, sitting on the
back doorstep, enjoying watching them play.

When they'd gone I asked one of the team who the little girl
was as her face was familiar but I couldn't quite place her. "It's
Thanda who arrived two weeks ago," they said, and suddenly I
remembered the day she arrived.

I had taken a group of people on a tour and we'd gone into
a cluster where Thanda's new home was. The other little girls in
her house came running over to say the new girl had bitten them,
drawing blood. I told them they must love her and turn the other
cheek, which of course wasn't what they wanted to hear. I went
in to Thanda's room to talk to her and she cowered in the corner
as though she was about to be punished. Instead I went over and
told her how pleased and excited I was that she'd come to LIV
and told her we loved her. She pushed me away and ran out of the
house like a frightened animal. I felt so sad for all she'd suffered in
her life that made her so scared and broken, and I knew that God
had handpicked her for the village and that she was on a path to
healing and wholeness.

Now I could barely recognise Thanda as the same girl who
had happily walked into my house, made herself at home and
played so well with the other children. "That is why you're here,"
I heard God say, "You're here for the one. Each child counts."

Then I knew we were here for good; this was our home.
Every morning I opened the curtains in our bedroom, looked
at the view over the houses of Cluster 5 and saw their washing

hanging on the line. It was a beautiful sight. At the beach house I would have complained about being able to see my neighbour's washing from my window and would have considered building higher walls so my view wasn't impaired. Here it represented life and reminded me that we were living in community; I wouldn't change it for anything.

Although there are many challenges of living in community we've learnt to love it, and it is such a huge privilege to be called by God to share in the lives of these children and mothers. God changes each of us as we live life together; for our part we know we will never be the same again.

One of the hardest things was moving away from our biological children and grandchildren. God was making us one family with everyone at LIV, but we knew this would have an impact on our own families. Although the village is only half an hour away, it was enough of a distance that we could no longer easily pop in on one another. When we told them they were shocked, and our daughter Kate wept, but their support was unconditional and selfless. We didn't want them to feel any less loved just because God had called us to love others too and we committed to still seeing them regularly and being present in their lives. We wanted to still be able to pick our grandchildren up from school and help out when needed. The highlight of our week is taking the two youngest grandchildren, Molly and Jack, out for pizza and milkshakes, and we love it when our eldest grandson, Ben, comes to visit and spends his time running around and enjoying himself with all the friends he's made among the village children.

ACTS 2

Tich

None of our staff had lived in the village, but soon after we moved to the farmhouse, they began to ask if they too could move on to LIV. It was wonderful to have so many commit not just to working at LIV but to giving their whole lives and it's a huge blessing to the mothers and the children. It really makes us feel like one big family that is truly committed to one another. Many of the children have never really received love or known how to give love in an appropriate way. They've often experienced impure and abusive relationships, but with the LIV team they begin to see and learn what real, committed love is all about. I had felt God was saying we couldn't ask other people to do what we weren't prepared to do ourselves so our move had pioneered the way for others.

I had been spending a lot of time reading about the early church and asking God if we would ever see the power that was prevalent in that church again. I began to challenge the staff living in the village that this could be an opportunity for God to set us apart and resurrect the Acts 2 church but we couldn't have one foot in the kingdom and one foot in the world.

A few months prior to Christmas, a city project in Cottonlands that had employed 20 local women collapsed. The project leaders asked us to take the women onto the village as workers in the fields, and they would pay their salaries. In the November they notified us that they were unable to continue to pay these salaries.

I asked God to provide for those women and he said, "You've got the money." He said to go back to the Acts 2 description of the church which says that those who had, shared with those who didn't have. I challenged our staff team to contribute towards the salaries of these ladies so they could continue to work, and amazingly they gave almost exactly what was needed. I was particularly touched by one young guy who gave 20 per cent of his salary. Between us we were able to pay two months' worth of salaries, by which time the city was in a position to start paying the women again.

God honoured the faithfulness and generosity of his people, and we could see he was really starting to do something in us as a church. We realised that LIV and everything we are doing is being the church. This is what church is supposed to look like.

For me, I knew that God was continuing to break my heart for those who are poverty-stricken. It was a process he had begun in Amaoti but he was continuing to soften my heart and show me that we needed to share with those in need in every way. I discovered that working with the poverty-stricken takes a lot of patience and long suffering. To disciple someone means walking a long road with them. Many times when things got hard at the village it was tempting to run away, but we would look into the faces of the children and know we could never leave them just as Jesus would never leave us. He's in it for the long haul and we need to be too.

I was inspired by Bill Hybels talking about the church in Acts 2. He heard a lecturer talking of the radical love shared by those who lived together in community, sharing their joy and sorrow, living openly and honestly before one another as they sought to serve God. He said,

> Those who had more shared freely with those who had less until socioeconomic barriers melted away. Masks came off as people related together in ways that bridged gender and racial chasms, and celebrated cultural differences. Acts 2 tells us that this community of believers, this church, offered unbelievers a vision of life that was so beautiful it took their breath away. It was so bold, so creative, so dynamic that they couldn't resist it.[1]

That was the kind of community we wanted to create; one that reflected the early church and therefore reflected God's love to all who saw it. We wanted to share with one another so that no one had need of any kind whether physical, spiritual or emotional.

SUCCESS TO SIGNIFICANCE

God also began to speak to me about the difference between success and significance. I had tasted my share of worldly success when I was playing sport at the highest level, but I had seen for myself it doesn't fulfil you. A famous film star once said that fame and fortune is like a mirage in the desert: you strive all your life to get there but when

---

1   Bill Hybels, *Courageous Leadership* (Grand Rapids, MI: Zondervan, 2009), 17–18.

you do, there is nothing. I had experienced this myself and realised there had to be more to life than success. I understand now that it was significance and not success that would fill the emptiness I was feeling.

Success, God showed me, is all about "me" whilst significance is about putting others first. Success usually looks good on the outside whereas significance has meaning on the inside. Many successful men and women seem to find favour with like-minded people, whereas significant people build bridges over divides with those who are not like them.

I am learning that it isn't successful people who will change the world. It is going to take the courageous who will take their eyes off just seeking success and focus on seeking significance as well. Significance for me was about coming to terms with my own brokenness which allowed me to understand the brokenness of others. You need a particular talent to be successful, but to be significant you only have to have a heart for others.

It's part of the DNA at LIV, in family life, in school and in church, that we instil in the children that life isn't about what you get, it's about what you give. We teach them to be outward looking in everything from how they treat their siblings, to how they look after guests on the village, to how we can together bless the local community and those who are in need.

Chapter 15

LIFE IN THE VILLAGE

Prosperity in the eyes of God is a changed life.
Charles Mulli

Tich and Joan

Living in the village can feel like getting a glimpse of the kingdom of God. We are a community of believers from different denominations, different races and different backgrounds, representing the rainbow nation that Nelson Mandela had so longed for. The children say we are all different shades of brown, calling us their peach Gogo and Baba while they see themselves as chocolate brown. When we say the Lord's Prayer we ask God for his kingdom to come and his will to be done on earth as it is in heaven. It's a small piece of heaven on earth to see broken lives restored, to live in a community of love and to be one family under our Father God.

There are so many things we love about life at LIV. One of our favourite times of day is when the children have finished school and they come and play outside their houses. We love to watch them having fun, though our hearts are in our mouths when they climb the tall mango trees! Village life is quite simple as we long for the children to have a healthy upbringing. They don't watch TV during the day, so they play outdoors for hours on end, and we don't allow them to have mobile phones. (We of course make provision for each child to contact family off the village where appropriate but we can see the way social media and constant Internet access is damaging young people around the world and we don't want to expose them to that when it's unnecessary.)

Seeing children who have come from such difficult circumstances able to play and enjoy life as children should, without fear of abuse and neglect, is one of the most satisfying pleasures you can possibly imagine. We love to watch them grow and develop their skills and can already recognise there are future farmers, mechanics, teachers, nurses, chefs, engineers, musicians, and even a couple of potential South African presidents among them!

CHANGED LIVES

Sipho was five years old when he arrived at LIV and he was physically underdeveloped due to neglect. He had been left sitting too much as a toddler, and so his core muscles hadn't developed properly. His body wasn't able to sweat, he was unable to run, and he would cry when Chester tried to coach him in sports. "I can't do it, coach," he would say after taking a few little steps and then coming to a halt. Over the following months Chester and the team worked closely with him. One of our occupational therapists saw him every day and helped him work on his core muscles. Within a year of being in the village Sipho ran four kilometres (around two and a half miles) without stopping! Everyone at LIV was talking about this incredible achievement and rejoicing with him; what a celebration! Now he is known as the boy who runs *everywhere*. With the right help he was able to overcome the disadvantages of his childhood and it swells our hearts every time we see him running past.

Jabulani came to us as a young boy who had been living on the streets. His LIV mother often found him sleeping outside on the veranda instead of in his new bed. Jabulani would steal things and hide them in his pillowcase, and when caught he would run away. Each time we would go and fetch him. On one occasion a board member was visiting us and when we took her for a walk around the village, Jabulani went into our house and stole her wallet out of her bag. Some of the other boys who were with him came and told us and brought it back minus R20. Jabu was nowhere to be found. After a long search of the property we reported him missing to the police.

A few days later his social worker gave us the name of an old man who had cared for Jabu off and on, and told us where we could find him. We found the old man and, to our great relief, Jabu was with him. He had used the R20 to catch a taxi to the Verulam police station, where he told them he was lost and asked them to give him a lift back to his community. We hugged him, looked into his face and told him we loved him like a son and we would keep on coming to fetch him. That day the penny finally dropped that someone really loved him and Jabu started to change.

Progress was slow, sometimes with two steps forward and three steps back. One day Stephen Lungu came to talk to the children and staff in the village. Stephen had been a street boy in Zimbabwe, ending up in an orphanage where he was beaten mercilessly every day, and later becoming a feared gang leader. He went to a crusade in Harare where he and his gang intended to cause havoc, but where he ended up giving his life to Jesus. Stephen had a huge impact on Jabu that day. It was the major turning point for him, and he kept asking his teacher to read the part in Stephen's book, *Out of the Black Shadows*, where he would rummage through the rubbish bins looking for something to eat.

Jabu began to settle down to village life and we began to notice he was a good runner. Our sports coaches started to train him and he was recently chosen to represent KwaZulu-Natal in the interschools cross country athletics championships in the Eastern Cape. We are so proud of him and where he has come from, and we know he is going to go far in life. Once more we were reminded that love never fails.

FAMILY CELEBRATIONS

Christmas Day at LIV is something special. We start the celebrations by gathering together for a worship service to honour Jesus and reflect on his birth. Then every family brings a contribution to our Christmas lunch and we eat a huge variety of foods from traditional turkey, to incredible African dishes cooked by the mothers. We lay out tables under the mango trees so we can take shade from the heat of the sun and enjoy a fine feast. After lunch the mothers give their children a gift and we give the mothers a gift. The kids often make cards for us and the mothers present us with a gift on behalf of them all. The kids run around laughing and playing together and it's wonderful to celebrate Jesus together.

Because there are so many birthdays in the village we hold a birthday celebration once a month, gathering together in the village square to have a meal and to dance together. In the early years we used to picnic in front of the farmhouse and dance on the lawn. We would park one of the village vehicles nearby, using the headlights to light up the area and the sound system to supply the music. These times created great unity and a sense of family and belonging. Today, with over 250 of us living in the village, we use the hall which has its own sound system, and the village square where we make pizzas in a huge pizza oven that we constructed out of the ruins of an old building. These times continue to be a highlight at LIV as we celebrate the goodness and provision of our God, but we never forget those small beginnings on the lawn.

GIVING BACK TO THE COMMUNITY

The children have everything they need and it's important that they learn to give back to the community. On Nelson Mandela's birthday, 18th July, South Africa honours our former president by giving time to serve others in less fortunate circumstances. This has become a wonderful tradition and many companies come to LIV to serve us by planting trees, harvesting bananas or helping out with other tasks that need doing around the village.

In turn we teach our children that it's not all about receiving but about giving, so we make peanut butter sandwiches (what else!) and take them to the children in the neighbouring Cottonlands school. The children hand out the food and interact with the pupils, which teaches them to share what they have and to look out for the needs of others.

We want to plant these seeds in our children from a young age so that giving is second nature to them and so they know you are never too young or too poor to make a difference in someone else's life. Giving also eradicates the spirit of entitlement that can so easily grow when we are given plenty. Learning to celebrate together as well as serve together is key as we all work to restore the lives of the children of LIV and prepare them to be released as stars and the future leaders of our country.

CHALLENGES

Though we see glimpses of God's kingdom, we also know the reality that until Jesus returns we will still have to do battle with earthly difficulties and challenges. One of the toughest things for us is that living in the village means we're available to people 24-7 and it can be hard to take a break. We try to be intentional and take time out, but things often crop up and our planned time off doesn't quite work out. The mothers each have a weekend off a month, and we encourage the staff to take at least a day off a week and to get off the village to have a break, plus the staff live at the top of the village, where the children are asked not to go, in order to give them some privacy and boundaries.

Living in the centre of the village and right by the offices means we're easily accessible to the children, the mothers, the staff and volunteers. We often have teams coming from around South Africa or from abroad who want to hear more about the village and to serve, and we always want to provide them with a warm welcome too, making it difficult to rest. After renting out our beach house for a year we decided to use it as a place of refuge so we can occasionally escape for some downtime. On the village, your life isn't your own.

One thing we hadn't been entirely prepared for was the number of electricity cuts. The first time it happened when we were living in the village the power was out for a few days. The darkness at night was all-consuming and very frightening for the children. We tried to eat the fruit and yoghurt in our fridge and nearly vomited because it had gone off so badly. All around the village, the meat and other food in fridges was rotting and being wasted. We began to see just a glimpse of life through the eyes of those who are poverty-stricken. When you can afford to replace the food then a power cut is frustrating, when that food is all you have and you don't know where the next meal is coming from, it's another story altogether.

Of course, we're not saying we experience these things in the same way or to the same degree but you see new levels of what people go through and it breaks your heart even more. When you are part of a relatively wealthy church you can often feel like there's not that much you can do to help those in poverty. When you see things from the other side you understand that if we all connected with just one family and helped provide them with a good meal once a week, that would make a huge difference to that family's life. There is so much that we so easily take for granted.

Tich

One of the privileges that is also a challenge is being there for the children and the community in times of crisis. When one of the Cottonlands community members who worked in our fields was stabbed, we went to visit him in hospital as he had no one else. It's an honour to be trusted by someone and to be there for them.

Taking one of our little boys, Lindelani, to the emergency dentist was quite an incredible experience for me too. He had an abscess, but was refusing to go as he was so scared. When the social worker went to get him from school he ran away. I found Lindelani and asked him if he would go to the dentist if I went with him and promised no one would hurt him. He agreed and when we got there they said they needed to take the tooth out. As they injected the anaesthetic he clung to me as though his life depended on it. They pulled and pulled and couldn't get the tooth out, while he screamed non-stop.

After half an hour I was crying with him and neither of us could take any more. I had promised him that no one was going to hurt him and felt I had let him down. I told them they had to stop and they had to do something else. They told me the only other option was to remove it surgically, which I asked them to do. The day after the operation I opened my door at 5 a.m. to find

Lindelani waiting outside the house wanting to say thank you for looking after him. I wept. He was longing to belong, longing to be looked after, and it was an honour to be there for him. He's a beautiful boy, a real leader with such a special heart. When people become your family there is a trust and stability because they know you won't ever leave them.

Tich and Joan

One of the saddest times for us was when we had to let five of our older teenage girls leave LIV over a short period of time. We try to give each child an appropriate amount of freedom and they receive much more than if they were in a government institution, where they need to be locked in at night. Our village has a guard at the entrance to ensure the safety of everyone inside, so we are able to allow the children to roam around quite freely as permitted by their mother. Unfortunately, that amount of freedom is not right for everyone.

As the children reach their teenage years we spend a lot of time sharing with them about their future, instilling hope in them, developing their God-given talents and encouraging them to dream and plan for their future. We also emphasise how the choices they make now will have consequences—for good and bad—on their future.

As we have said, one of the tragedies for many who grow up in poverty-stricken communities is that they have very little hope which causes them to live for the day rather than to think long term. We try to help them see that we are fully committed to them, that they can choose to grow up and even get married at the village if they so wish, so they know we are in it for the long haul. When they start to absorb this, they begin to think differently about the way they behave in the present.

Many teens and pre-teens living in poverty start having sex with multiple partners from an early age and end up with a string of babies before they reach their 20s, but we teach our teenagers about healthy boundaries and godly living which includes not being sexually promiscuous. These are the guidelines we ask them to live by in order to have a healthy and safe environment for everyone in the village, but of course every person reaches an age where they have the freedom to choose whether to live this way or not.

These particular girls obviously didn't want to be in the village anymore and were causing havoc, refusing to stay in their homes, harassing the other children, and breaking into empty houses. We ended up in the gutting position of having to work with their external social workers to find them alternative placements, either with extended family members or individual foster families.

When this happened with a number of girls in a row we were hit with the stark realisation that LIV is not going to be the right place for every child and that was incredibly painful. All we could do was let them go and pray that the seeds sown in their lives would bear fruit. We all experienced a time of grieving, especially their house mothers, as we said goodbye.

At times like this you have to grieve the loss but try to hold on to the good news of all the lives you *are* seeing changed. We've seen so many of our teenagers go through a process of realising that they can go back out into the community and make a positive difference. You try and remember that if you can even impact one person's life for the better, they can go on to bless someone else who can bless someone else and so the cycle goes on. There is a ripple effect when we invest in people and we may never get to see the results this side of heaven, we just have to keep loving and serving faithfully.

Chapter 16

EIGHT WEDDINGS AND THREE FUNERALS

Rejoice with those who rejoice; mourn with those who mourn.

Romans 12:15

Joan

Living as a family means seeing all aspects of life, both in its joys and in its sorrows. With lots of young volunteers and staff coming and going there is often romance in the air, and we've seen no fewer than eight couples get married over the past two years.

One of the most special started when Carita, a beautiful young Afrikaans lady who had previously worked with Watoto, arrived in the village in 2012. God had spoken to her about coming to work at LIV so she obediently packed up her worldly belongings and came to us, soon becoming a core part of the team. A year or so later a teacher and sports coach called Jonathan arrived from Liverpool in the UK planning on serving us for a year. Jonathan fell instantly in love with the vivacious Carita and confided in us that he believed God had told him she was to be his wife. Unfortunately, she found him to be an arrogant English man—even worse, a Liverpool football supporter! The more he tried to win Carita's heart, the harder things became between them.

Eventually Jonathan's year was up and he had given up hope of winning Carita over. He came to see us and said that he realised God had told him to come to LIV but hadn't told him to leave. He felt it would be disobedient to return to England and asked if he could stay and continue to work with the children. We were delighted, as we loved having him on the team, but needed to check he wasn't just staying because of Carita. He assured us he'd let that go as Carita was showing no signs of interest in being anything more than friends. We chatted some more and agreed he would stay on indefinitely. Just as he left the farmhouse, his phone beeped. It was a text from Carita asking if they could chat as she'd had a change of heart. God had been waiting for Jonathan to realise he was called to LIV before he began a relationship with Carita, and now that he knew he was staying for the right reasons, a relationship blossomed.

It was a whirlwind romance and within a year they were married right here in the village with Tich officiating. When it came time for him to give the groom some words of wisdom Tich said, "When Jesus was confronted with difficult questions he often said nothing. My advice to you, Jonathan, when you are faced with tricky situations, just say nothing." Sound advice indeed!

Everyone was invited to join the celebration and what a day it was. One of the young boys arrived two hours early; he'd never been to a wedding and didn't want to miss it! During the ceremony five or six of the children came right up to the front to sit near Jonathan and Carita's feet so they wouldn't miss a minute of the action. The mothers sang and the kids did Zulu dances; everyone had a wonderful time. Jonathan and Carita stayed living in the village after their wedding and are now expecting their first child, who will be coming on the first ever LIV Youth Ambassadors Choir tour to Europe as his mother is the coordinator of the whole thing!

RELEASING OUR FIRST LIV STARS

When we began LIV we hadn't planned on taking in any special needs children as we felt we didn't have the facilities to look after them. But in 2012 a babies' home in Durban North closed and asked us to take their children, including two severely disabled cerebral palsy children, Sibisuso and Khetiwe, aged six and seven.

When we went to visit them we knew instantly that God wanted us to take them into the village. The lady at the home said there were no good facilities for them elsewhere so we prayed if we could ask any of our mothers to take them on. I felt God show me to ask Mama Dudu, who had herself raised a daughter with cerebral palsy. Tragically her daughter had died at the age of 10 and I didn't know how to ask her to go through the same trauma with another child. Amazingly when I spoke to her she said God had been preparing her heart and she felt like these were her children to love and look after. "These are the children of my heart," she told me.

Sibisuso and Khetiwe moved into her home and became part of her family. They received amazing love and care from Dudu's entire family, including their new brothers and sisters, and Dudu received extra support from the other mothers and the occupational therapists. In fact, the whole village adored Sibisuso and Khetiwe, and they got more attention than any of the other children!

In 2014 Sibisuso was in incredible pain from a dislocated hip that an operation hadn't been able to fix. The doctors couldn't make him comfortable and sadly the Lord took him home. The entire village mourned his passing and attended the first funeral we'd held at the village. Our heart had always been to release the children like stars, we just never thought we'd release our first star directly to heaven. We wept for weeks.

Six months later our precious Khetiwe joined Sibisuso. That morning her caregiver in the day centre had heard her giggling and turned around. Khetiwe only giggled that way when someone was tickling her, but there was no one in sight. At that moment, Khetiwe took her last breath and we knew the angels had come to take her to be with Jesus.

We had longed for both children to receive healing on this earth but God's ways are not always our ways, and their healing came when they went to their heavenly home. It comforts us to know they are free from their earthly pain and we're sure they are dancing with joy in God's presence. All we were able to do was love them with his love and for a short time we were privileged to have them with us. We built a garden of remembrance overlooking Hazelmere dam and we scattered their ashes there so we'd all have a place to go and remember these two children who touched our hearts so deeply.

OUR MR. DUPS

In 2014 we were joined by a new high school teacher, Mr. Dups. He was in his late 50s and he told us he was a backslidden Christian, having been disappointed by the church. We loved his honesty and encouraged him to get close to Jesus again and watched in amazement as his life changed. He was a real blessing to our teenagers, full of passion and compassion and keen to do everything he could to help them learn. He thought out of the box, taking the children out to the LIV factory or into the fields and gardens to teach them, and he loved taking the classes on field trips outside of the village too. Everyone loved him; he had such a wonderful sense of humour and nothing was too much for him, he was always happy to help anyone in need.

Mr. Dups had always had heart problems and a year later, the day before school started and one week before his 60th birthday, he had a heart attack in his classroom whilst preparing for his students. He went to be with the Lord. The week before he had told one of the staff that when he arrived at LIV he was on the bottom rung of the ladder with his Christian walk but said, "I've reached the top rung and I'm ready to go home now."

Once more the village came together as a family and even in these painful valley moments we were able to teach the children that death is a part of life, that it is right to grieve and mourn but God promises that joy comes in the morning. We celebrated these lives with joy and sorrow; two emotions that seem to mingle often as we do life together in all its forms. We realised once more that LIV is not just for broken children but also for broken adults who are themselves children of the living God. He sends us different people for different reasons and he clearly sent Mr. Dups to be restored to Jesus before he went home. He was another star released into heaven.

Chapter 17

A FIVE-YEAR CELEBRATION

"Not by might nor by power, but by my Spirit," says the Lord.

Zechariah 4:6

Joan

After the banquet where we fed 4,000 people, many said, "Why don't we make this an annual event? When will the next one be?" "Not in my lifetime!" was always my response. But in 2015, five years after we started the village, we wanted to do something to celebrate the milestone. God had shown himself to be so faithful and had provided so incredibly for the village over those five years that we wanted to honour him.

Rather than try and feed thousands of people in one go—which would quite possibly have sent me to an early grave—we held a number of events. The first was a banquet on a Thursday night for 700 people who had supported us and LIV on our journey. At the first ICC banquet we had shared a crazy vision; now we could invite people to come to the village to see for themselves how they had helped make that dream a reality. We held a three-course dinner in our hall, with Shaun Pollock as our MC. The same three people who had spoken at our ICC banquet did so again here: Rory Dyer and Dr. Zweli Mkhize, along with Tich sharing about what God had done in the previous five years and all that we were looking forward to in the future. He shared our heart to see many villages across South Africa, and ultimately across the whole of Africa, caring for the continent's millions of neglected orphans and vulnerable children. Though it once again felt like a crazy vision, God kept reminding us not to limit him, but just to listen and follow where he led. At the first banquet the Watoto choir from Uganda had entertained the guests; this time, five years later, we had our own choir of LIV mothers and children who celebrated and entertained us. There wasn't a dry eye in the place as they sang of the greatness of our God.

The following morning we held a breakfast in the city for the business people who weren't able to make it out to the village. Bob Johnson from Bethel Church in Redding, California, and Stephen Lungu, CEO of African Enterprise, addressed the 500 men and women who attended. That evening we invited the youth from various churches around Durban to join us for an evening of celebration and worship.

Finally, on the Saturday morning we hosted 550 ladies for a lavish tea party. The ladies came from churches far and wide, and we invited all the mothers of LIV, the women who work in our fields and those on our staff team. As always, our desire was to do everything with excellence to glorify God, and so we paid particular attention to the small details that would make it a truly special occasion. The hall was decorated beautifully, and the tables were set with flowers and a little gift for each guest to remind her that she is the fragrance of God.

We had ordered a selection of delicious cakes, muffins and fruit skewers but on the day of the tea, as Dr. Gerlinde was helping the caterer to put the cakes on the tables, she realised they were running out. "Don't worry, I've brought exactly enough for all 50 tables," the caterer assured her. Gerlinde's heart sank to the floor. "We added an extra five tables. No one told you, did they?" The caterer shook his head in horror. We weren't going to have enough to feed the 50 extra people. Gerlinde and the caterer panicked. Quietly, Gerlinde prayed, "God, we need your help and we need it now—do something!" She wished there had been time for her to get on her knees and pray more reverently and eloquently but people were due to arrive shortly and there was no time to spare. "What shall we do?" the caterer asked, white-faced. "Just keep putting them out," Gerlinde said. "Even though there aren't enough, just keep going."

They finished the first 50 tables and found something strange: there were more cakes in the boxes. They set up the next table and then the next and still there were more cakes. As they set up the last table they realised they had exactly the right amount. The caterer was wide-eyed; "How did that happen? I know I only brought enough for the 50 tables you ordered." "Don't try and work it out logically," Gerlinde replied, "God supplied our need. It's a shame we don't have fruit skewers for those last five tables, but at least they have the same amount of cakes as everyone else." The caterer picked up an empty box that had contained muffins, ready to throw it away, and gasped. "There are 50 fruit skewers in here! They're not ones I brought; they're not even in my packaging!" God had foreseen our need and got the angels baking and chopping fruit early that morning to provide the food we needed.

There was a heavenly spread that day; we had sought to honour God with a special tea to thank him publicly for the way that he provided and here he was, even providing the cake for us to enjoy.

A SELF-SUSTAINABLE FUTURE

Tich

After five years we had much to reflect on and be thankful for; we could see how far God had brought us and how he was preparing us for the future. We had wanted LIV to become self-sustaining so that its future wouldn't be solely dependent on donations, and we were beginning to see the potential emerging. Over the years God has blown us away with the businesses he has brought our way and the opportunities these have provided to invest in our workers and bring future profits back into the village to support the children.

When we first started talking about what kind of business we should open, Joan said to me, "All I know about is clothing." We agreed this was as good a place to start as any, so she bought back the machinery from the Circuit Sportswear factory she and Vin had set up in the 1980s. In August 2014 we opened a factory in the village, staffed by 35 previously unskilled trainees from the local community. The factory produces all our school uniforms and clothes for the village children, and has gradually developed to produce a range of LIV products including various fashion T-shirts, crafts and home-ware that we sell online. As the business grows, it will continue to train factory workers who will not only get an opportunity to be part of the manufacturing team that produce the LIV products for local and export markets but also have the possibility of working in other clothing factories around Durban, or even starting their own home based business.

LIV clothing is developing and producing a range of T-shirts and other products including accessories, homeware and crafts for local and export markets. We're excited that in 2016 our daughter, Kate, gave up her very lucrative career in the corporate world to join the LIV business team to develop the LIV clothing brand.

Even before the village began we dreamt about growing and selling cut flowers. LIV Flowers was our first business and is going from strength to strength as we provide flowers to outlets around the country. It is now the second biggest grower of anthuriums nation-wide, with the potential for export in the near future.

A young man, Patrick Mbokazi, came to us to do his practical course after graduating in agriculture at the University of KwaZulu-Natal, and is now heading up our new LIV agriculture business. LIV Hydroponics grows cucumbers in the newly built tunnels on the farm that are sold to leading supermarkets, and it has trained and employed a group of previously unemployed and unskilled men and women.

LIV also owns shares in a number of businesses doing everything from manufacturing sticky labels to offering industrial cleaning services. We have a 26 per cent stake in the Southern African arm of the second largest logistics company in the world; who would have thought that orphaned children would be the beneficiaries of a partnership with a worldwide company?

One opportunity we are hugely excited about is the development of LIV Moringa. Moringa trees are known as miracle trees because of the amazing medicinal value in the leaves and seeds. It has been scientifically proven it has more minerals and vitamins than any other plant. We have already planted over 100,000 trees on the farm and plan to plant a million trees over the next few years. The crushed leaves of the moringa plant are sold in powder and tablet form to various supermarkets and pharmacies and the pure oil from the moringa seeds can be used as a salad dressing, for cooking, and also for skin products and perfumes.

When we began LIV we always wondered how we were going to sustain the village, and as our hearts grew to see many such villages built around the country we knew they couldn't be funded by donations alone. As we look back we realise that God had it all planned out from the very beginning. It's astonishing to realise that the moringa product alone has the potential to sustain the whole village; we dream of being in a position to fund many, many villages so that every child across our country can have a home and a mother who loves them.

The businesses have also given us amazing opportunities to sow into people's lives, and give them chances to grow and develop. Each department at LIV has a mentoring programme to raise up those who are showing potential. One of these success stories is Lindiwe, who started as a worker in the fields. We noticed her potential as a leader and promoted her to manage the cleaning staff. We then discovered that she was passionate about cooking and were able to give her the opportunity to attend the LIV culinary school when it first opened. The school started with 20 students from the local community and is being run in partnership with the International Hotel School and a number of sponsors. The students spend six months doing theory and practical cooking lessons in the specially designed LIV kitchen and in the following six months they are able to get practical experience in various hotels and restaurants, qualifying at the end of the year with a nationally recognised certificate. There is a shortage of chefs in South Africa, which almost guarantees them opportunities in the workplace.

God said right from the start that people would come to us, see how things were working and ask why, and that we would be able to point them to Jesus. We wondered how we could ever do anything that would catch the attention of government, and now we work with them on a regular basis. We recently worked together to launch a health clinic for the community of Cottonlands who previously were visited once a week by a doctor, and they partnered with us to open the tunnels where we grow the cucumbers. On these projects we regularly cross paths with government officials, and many want to know how LIV has become the success that they see, and every time we always tell them the same answer: Jesus.

Chapter 18

A NEW SEASON BEGINS

See, I am doing a new thing! Now it springs
up; do you not perceive it?

Isaiah 43:19

Tich

We had often been asked about the succession plan for LIV and what would happen when we are no longer around. Our reply was always, "God has it all figured out and in his perfect time, he will show us." We have learnt to trust him to bring the right people along at the right time and he has sent some incredible young people to journey with us these past few years who we have been mentoring. In January 2014 God began to show me that we needed to particularly invest in our young leaders to raise them up and prepare them to take over the responsibility of the day-to-day running of the village.

Joan

Every Monday morning the entire village, including all the volunteers, staff, mothers and children, gather together as a family, to start the week giving thanks for what we have. It's a time when we often remind ourselves about the vision, share testimonies of God's goodness, and receive teaching. In October 2015, God put on our mentor Ann's heart to share the story of Moses and Joshua. Moses had been leading the people, but before they got to the Promised Land, God told Moses that he had chosen Joshua to take over and lead his people into this new season (Deut. 31:1–3).

God had rescued Moses from death as a child, restored his life, raised him up to be a leader and pioneer, and when he probably least expected it, he called him out of the lavish lifestyle he was living in Pharaoh's palace. He prepared him in the desert, finally releasing him to rescue, restore, raise and release the children of Israel who were in bondage and being abused. Moses was a flamboyant, wonderful character who was full of emotion and wore his heart on his sleeve. He often wrestled with God about the task set before him and how incapable he felt he was, but he never gave up. Tich is the Moses of LIV.

Joshua was very different to Moses, quietly confident and trusting that, no matter the giants, his Commander-in-Chief would always go before them and lead them in the right way. God didn't send Joshua into the new season alone but rallied a large team around him to cross over in unity, shoulder to shoulder.

We knew instantly that God was showing us it was time to pass the baton on. We also knew with absolute certainty that Chester, who had been leading our sports programme, was the Joshua and that he and his wife Athi, along with Jonathan and Carita, were the new leaders who would take on the management of the village in the next season. They have the same DNA as us, have embraced the vision and have let go of the material things of life. We have watched in awe as they have laid down their lives and surrendered all to serve Jesus by serving the children and mothers in the village.

In January 2016, at our annual LIV staff and volunteer training conference, we washed the feet of Chester, Athi, Jonathan and Carita and prayed over them, releasing the authority to them, and then invited the team, who would walk alongside them, to pray over them and stand with them in unity. It was a milestone moment that none of us will ever forget and we wept together as we each felt the tangible presence of the Holy Spirit.

NOW WHAT, LORD?

As I said earlier, when Tich told me in November 2012 that he felt God wanted us to leave our beach house and move onto the village, I said I would help him pack and visit him on weekends. Since moving to the village I had started saying to people, "If Tich says we can go back to the beach house, I will tell him I will help him pack and visit him on weekends." I had grown to love our farmhouse and said I was there for life, believing that one day my ashes would be scattered on the front lawn.

Tich had been saying to me that we needed to give the new leaders space and take time off the village. I realise now he was gently trying to tell me that we needed to move out of the farmhouse to make way for the new managers to live there. After my reaction to him three years before when he said we needed to leave our home and move into the farmhouse, he wasn't about to make the same mistake in coming straight out with it, and was waiting for God to show me!

Soon after we officially handed over the baton, I woke up early one morning and said out loud to God, "The farmhouse isn't mine, Lord, but yours. I give it back to you." It was as if scales fell off my eyes and I had a "light bulb" moment, just as Tich had hoped. I realised with sudden clarity that of course this house, in the centre of the village which everyone passes regularly, must always be where the village manager lives. We needed to move out so Chester, Athi and their two children could move in. I was reminded of the many times Tich says, "When you pass the baton you must let go completely otherwise the team cannot run the race." Once again I felt the incredible love and grace of my heavenly Father resting upon me as he gently prepared me for what he was about to do. I shed tears of joy and sorrow as I packed up our belongings and prepared to go back to the beach house.

As we look back at God's timeline we are astounded at his perfect and pre-ordained plan. He sends in the pioneers and builders and then the settlers and his timing is always perfect. In January 2002 I overcame my fear and went into Amaoti with peanut butter sandwiches for a handful of children. It was seven years later, in January 2009, that God said to Tich it was time for the village, and we were to pass the baton of Amaoti on to the young people we had raised up. Exactly seven years later again he was telling us to pass the baton on to the young people we have mentored at LIV, and to come aside for a season of rest and restoration as he prepares us for what's next.

We recognise that God has wired us to be pioneers, not long term managers. We believe we have done what God called and enabled us to do, to build and set up this first village, with Jesus Christ at the centre, to be a model for others to follow. We have also developed the LIV Ambassadors Choir, which we hope to take on tour to many parts of the world as one of the ways we raise awareness of, and support for, orphans and vulnerable children in South Africa and around the world.

God is beginning to whisper about villages in Gauteng and other parts of southern Africa too. The former premier of KwaZulu-Natal, Dr. Zweli Mkhize, recently took Tich up to a place called Ndumo to speak to the lady chief there who has land she wants to give us to set up a village. I said to Tich, "This time I will help you pack your bags and never visit you!" Ndumo is a five-hour drive from Durban on the border of Swaziland and Mozambique, where it is hot and dry and the temperature hits 40 degrees in the shade. I woke up one morning in a sweat having dreamt we were living there in a mud hut with no water or indoor toilet, and said to the Lord, "Surely that was just a dream brought on by eating pizza last night!"

God knows our limitations but he also knows we can do all things through Jesus, his Son, who strengthens us. We continue to journey with him and try not to limit him. But for now we actively rest with him as we wait for him to show us the next steps. He knows we will never say no to him, and we know he will continue to show us grace.

THE GOLDEN THREAD

Tich and Joan

We are overwhelmed by our Father's love for us; he has forgiven us so much and we find ourselves falling more and more in love with him every day. We pray that he will continue to break our hearts for the things that break his. As we look back at the journey of our lives, where he has brought us from, to where he has taken us over the past 15 years, starting with a group of caddies and sandwiches for starving children under a tree in Amaoti, to the establishment of the LIV village which a thousand children will call home, we see a golden thread of lives rescued, restored, raised and released, including ours, the children of LIV and many others along the way.

We feel humbled that God found us worthy to be entrusted with the lives of these precious children. We have never been busier, we have never had more problems, but there is no place we would rather be. It is the greatest privilege of our lives to play a small part in what we believe is God's plan for the orphaned and vulnerable children of our land. We look forward to watching him continue to transform their lives and release them into all he has planned and purposed for them. For now, we rest in his presence and we wait expectantly for the next season of the LIV journey, knowing it is all in his mighty hands.

AFTERWORD

They gave as much as they were able, and even beyond their
ability. Entirely on their own, they urgently pleaded with us for
the privilege of sharing in this service to the Lord's people.
2 Corinthians 8:3–4

There are five million orphaned children in South Africa, 50 million in Africa, and 150 million in the world, as well as untold millions of vulnerable children who are at risk daily. Jesus taught us to pray: "Your kingdom come and your will be done, on earth as it is in heaven." It was the simplest of prayers to remind us we should be seeking to make this world look a little bit more like heaven every day. As a friend said to us recently, "If heaven were to come to earth it would look like family." God's will is for all of us to care for the orphaned and vulnerable children in this world, to give them a family and a place to belong.

The church is God's answer. The church around the world has everything it needs to solve the current catastrophic situation and bring change on a large scale. There is only one problem. We are the church, and God doesn't have a plan B. It's time for us to rise up and become the church that Jesus prayed for. We need to be his hands and feet, showing the world that he cares about the widow, the orphan, the destitute and the poor. One Christian charity in the UK, Tearfund, used a poster of a child with the slogan, "I can't eat prayers". Many were offended by this but it was true; we can't glibly say we will pray for people who are suffering and then move on. We need to learn from the Good Samaritan that we should pray for people whilst we feed, clothe and, if need be, shelter them. It is time for us to stop being spectators in this dying world, get off the stands, join the team and get our hands dirty.

Richard Stearns, president of World Vision, once said that if we heard of a plane crashing and 260 lives lost, the whole world would mourn. TV news channels and newspapers would run the story for days and few hearts would be untouched at the tragedy of these lives being lost. Yet every day 26,000 children (the equivalent of 100 planes) die from starvation, lack of sanitation and inadequate healthcare in Africa, and it doesn't even make the news.[1]

It's not just children who are suffering; the whole world is in turmoil. There are wars and threats of terrorism, earthquakes, climate change wreaking havoc, an HIV/AIDS pandemic, rape, abuse, homelessness, and high rates of unemployment. There is huge disparity between the rich and the poor. The picture is bleak. Yet we have never been more excited about the opportunity for the church to awaken and be what God intended for it to be.

---

1   Richard Stearns, *The Hole in Our Gospel* (Nashville: Thomas Nelson, 2009), 106–7.

How do we do it? We start by taking the love God has put in our hearts and sharing it with a street child, a prostitute, a lonely neighbour, someone who is hungry. Many of us strive for fame, fortune, power and influence but so often we forget that in God's eyes the most important thing is how we look after those in need.

If we stay behind the walls of our churches people will die. Others will stay in a cycle of poverty that they will pass on to their own children after them because no one was willing to step in and empower them to change their lives. We need to hear God's heartbeat for those in poverty. We must allow him to soften our hearts where we've become immune to stories of suffering. And we need to act.

GOD'S PLAN FOR YOU

We wanted to write this book to tell you about God's grace and mercy. He brought us both from desperate places, places where we were trying to satisfy our own needs and had wound up in a mess. He rescued us, restored us, raised us and released us and we believe he wants to do the same for you. He has changed our lives and he can change yours.

But we've learnt he doesn't just bless us for our own sake, he blesses us so that we can bless others. That's our story and that's the story of the church; we are here to testify through our words and deeds that there is a loving God and he is as real to us as breathing. Walking in the supernatural power of his Holy Spirit, the very same Spirit who raised Jesus from the dead and who now lives in us, allowing him to lead, guide and teach us, has become the most natural thing for us. He is the same yesterday, today and forever. He sees all things, knows all things, owns all things and he is certainly coming back soon, as he promised, to re-establish heaven on earth. If he hasn't returned before our time is up, we know the moment we take our last breath on this earth we will be with him face to face in heaven and we will return with him when he returns. Until then we continue to love and serve in his name.

If you've read this story and think, "I could never do that" then we've failed. We want you to close these pages thinking, "If God can help orphans and vulnerable children through those two old ducks imagine what he can do through me?" Don't wait till you're older; don't wish you were younger. Don't think you need more qualifications, more money or more time. Don't think God wants to wait until you're perfect (surely we've convinced you he uses imperfect people!). Don't think you need to know the end when you begin. God doesn't show us the whole picture; he knew we'd have been too petrified to take even the first step. But as we say yes, he shows us the plans he has for us bit by bit.

We often picture God the Father, Jesus the Son and the Holy Spirit having a conversation asking, "Who can we get to build villages to look after our precious orphaned children?" We imagine the Son saying, "I can see Tich and Joan Smith waving their arms; I think they're willing." The Father replies, "Is there really no one else?" "No, Dad. No one else is foolish enough to do it." If we think we know it all, God struggles to use us as we want to do everything our own way. When we know we're weak and we're broken, we know the only way to get his plan done is to rely fully on him and to allow his strength to shine through. We've made more mistakes than anyone and we have no qualifications to do what we do except for the fact that we love the Lord, and he has broken our hearts for the things that break his. By his grace he has used our lives for his glory.

God has a purpose for you. He put this book in your hands for a reason. We pray he has planted a seed in your heart and that he will water it. We pray you will find opportunities in front of you to love others and that you'll see them for what they are even if they are small moments of kindness. When we don't feel like we have much to give, we have to remember that God is in the business of multiplication. Look at your hands. What do you already have? What gifts, talents, skills and resources do you have that God can use? He fed 4,000 with a boy's packed lunch; what more could he do through you? Start with a kind word, a helping hand, a peanut butter sandwich. If we all gave as we were able, all those little bits would add up to a changed world.

Say yes to God and know that as you give him your heart he is able to do more than you ask or dare to imagine. God uses those who say, "Yes, Lord, send me."

APPENDIX 1

FIND OUT MORE ABOUT LIV

If you'd like to find out all the latest LIV news, you can head to www.liv-village.com. There you can check out the latest videos and blogs, shop for our branded merchandise and sign up to be on our mailing list.

SOCIAL MEDIA

www.facebook.com/livvillage
www.twitter.com/LIV_Village
www.youtube.com/user/livvillage
Instagram: LIV-Village

GET INVOLVED

LIV VOLUNTEER PROGRAMME

We work with hundreds of volunteers each year from all over the world who come either on their own or as a group from a church, school or business. The vision of LIV is enhanced by the active participation of volunteers and we are so grateful for people travelling from different places to serve the mothers and children. Volunteers can come for as little as a week or for more than a year, and they have the option of staying on the village in our volunteer accommodation.

When you apply we create a volunteer itinerary based on your age, skills and how long you'll be staying with us. Volunteers under the age of 18 need to be accompanied by an adult.

For further information and to apply for the volunteer programme, you can go online or email info@liv-village.com.

LIV CORPORATE DAYS

Coming to LIV can be a life-changing corporate team building day. The focus is on physical tasks of various degrees—from building fences to planting trees, from painting and decorating houses to covering library books—as well as interaction with the children. As part of the LIV corporate day service we provide an experienced motivational speaker who partners with LIV and who creates specific packages to suit your company's needs, and includes team building games.

For further information and to book a day, email info@liv-village.com.

GAP YEAR—LIV4CHANGE

LIV4Change exists to help young people deepen their walk with Christ by revealing and restoring identity, providing intentional discipleship and active internship work, and giving the opportunity to serve the vision and community of LIV. Each young person on the programme will take part in three months of discipleship, followed by three months of an internship and work experience in a selected area. LIV4Change includes teaching, pastoral counselling and mentoring. We believe this gap year provides a fresh way for young people to thrive, see their potential and be given a platform to change lives around them. LIV4Change demonstrates the "upside down" kingdom of God, whereby in giving, God's children receive much more. The course runs from January to June.

Apply by email: info@liv-village.com.

APPENDIX 2

THE PREMIER'S OFFICE
IHHOVISI LIKANDUNAKULU
PROVINCE OF KWAZULU-NATAL   ISIFUNDAZWE SAKWAZULU-NATALI

5th Floor, 300 Langalibalele Street (Longmarket), Pietermaritzburg, 3201
PO Box 412, Pietermaritzburg, 3200
Tel: +27 (0) 33 341 3329/3335 Fax: +27 (0) 33 342 7368

To Whom it may Concern,

RE: Letter of Support for the Lungisisa Indlela Village, KwaZulu-Natal

I write this letter which confirms that the KZN Provincial Government fully supports the LIV project outside Veralum in Cottonlands KZN. We are partnering with LIV and have identified this as one of our "Pilot Projects"

The KZN Provincial Government has been involved in this initiative since its inception. It was launched at the ICC on 7th April 2010, and it is a partnership between the Church, the Government and Private Business. The concept of these villages is to look after widows, orphans and vulnerable children who are suffering largely through the HIV/AIDS pandemic which has devastated our province. We see this as a possible solution to this massive problem, and we have pledged our support in assisting LIV in any way in which we can, to make sure this project becomes a reality.

The comment period for the attached Draft Basic Assessment Report (Ref No. DM/007/10) is forty (40) days and I would request that every effort is made by your department to respond to the Environmental Practitioner and competent Authority with the shortest timeframe possible.

I know that you are all extremely busy, but your assistance and input into the review and comment on this application is greatly appreciated.

Yours sincerely

Dr Z.L. Mkhize
Premier: KwaZulu-Natal
Date: 01/03/2011